Windows for the Oracle DBA
The Definitive Reference

Oracle In-Focus Series

Mark Sorger

"Your only job security is between your ears."

- Thomas J. Sorger

Windows for the Oracle DBA
The Definitive Reference

By Mark Sorger

Oracle In-focus Series: Book 44
Series Editor: Donald K. Burleson
Production Manager: Robin Rademacher and Jennifer Stanley
Production Editor: Valerre Aquitaine
Cover Design: Janet Burleson
Printing History: February 2013 for First Edition

ISBN 10: 0-9776715-1-8
ISBN 13: 978-0-9776715-1-9
Library of Congress Control Number: 2013931103

Table of Contents

Using the Online Code Depot

Purchase of this book provides complete access to the online code depot that contains sample code scripts. Any code depot scripts in this book are located at the following URL in zip format and ready to load and use:

rampant.cc/windows.htm

If technical assistance is needed with downloading or accessing the scripts, please contact Rampant TechPress at rtp@rampant.cc.

Conventions Used in this Book

It is critical for any technical publication to follow rigorous standards and employ consistent punctuation conventions to make the text easy to read. However, this is not an easy task. With database terminology there are many types of notation that can confuse a reader. For example, some Oracle utilities such as STATSPACK and TKPROF are always spelled in CAPITAL letters, while Oracle parameters and procedures have varying naming conventions in the database documentation. It is also important to remember that many database commands are case sensitive, are always left in their original executable form and never altered with italics or capitalization. Hence, all Rampant TechPress books follow these conventions:

- **Parameters:** All database parameters will be lowercase italics. Exceptions to this rule are parameter arguments that are commonly capitalized (KEEP pool, TKPROF); these will be left in ALL CAPS.

- **Variables:** All procedural language (e.g. PL/SQL) program variables and arguments will also remain in lowercase italics (*dbms_job*, *dbms_utility*).

- **Tables & dictionary objects:** All data dictionary objects are referenced in lowercase italics (*dba_indexes*, *v$sql*). This includes all *v$* and *x$* views (*x$kcbcbh*, *v$parameter*) and dictionary views (*dba_tables*, *user_indexes*).

- **SQL:** All SQL is formatted for easy use in the code depot, and all SQL displayed in lowercase. The main SQL terms (select, from, where, group by, order by, having) will always appear on a separate line.

- **Programs & Products:** All products and programs that are known to the author are capitalized according to the vendor specifications (CentOS, VMware, Oracle, etc.). All names known by Rampant TechPress to be trademark names appear in this text as initial caps. References to UNIX are always made in uppercase.

Acknowledgements

This type of highly technical reference book requires the dedicated efforts of many people. Even though I am the author, my work ends when I deliver the content. After each chapter is delivered, several Oracle DBAs carefully review and correct the technical content. After the technical review, experienced copy editors polish the grammar and syntax.

The finished work is then reviewed as page proofs and turned over to the production manager, who arranges the creation of the online code depot and manages the cover art, printing distribution, and warehousing.

In short, the author plays a small role in the development of this book, and I need to thank and acknowledge everyone who helped bring this book to fruition:

- **Robin Rademacher and Jennifer Stanley** for the production management including the coordination of the cover art, page proofing, printing, and distribution.

- **Valerre Q Aquitaine** for help in the production of the page proofs.

- **Janet Burleson** for exceptional cover design and graphics.

- **John Lavender** for assistance with the web site, and for creating the code depot and the online shopping cart for this book.

- **Don Burleson** for providing me with the opportunity to write this book.

With my sincerest thanks,

Mark Sorger

Preface

This book is not intended to be a complete manual on Windows Server Administration; there are dozens of those already out there that were written by individuals with far more knowledge of the subject than I will ever possess.

Instead, this book is a summary of the knowledge that I have gained over the years working with Oracle on Windows Servers: the quirks, the gotchas, the things I had to dig to figure out. The intent is to show what is possible, to be used as a springboard for your further research. After all, nobody's requirements are exactly the same, but knowing something is possible to do, and having a starting point on how to do it, goes a long way towards helping you build the best solutions for your situation. That starting point is what I am hoping to give you here.

In Windows, there are several ways to do the same thing. The ways shown in the book are the ways I do those things, but there may be several other ways to do the same thing. Pick the ones you like!

I started with Oracle first on VAX/VMS, and then moved on to Oracle on HP/UX, so believe me when I tell you that running Oracle on Windows was a new experience to me as well. The things that assisted me were a prior background as a programmer and server administrator, as well as a then newly-earned certification in Windows NT Server. I already knew what needed to be done, and so do you – backups, exports, batch jobs, installs, upgrades, etc. The question was how, since there was no *crontab*, no *vi*, no *grep*, and no *mailx*. Over time, however, I figured it out as I needed to.

I have taken what I have since learned over the years from "the school of hard knocks" (as my Dad used to say) and tried to capture the best of those in this book. If you learn how to do just one new thing that you could not do before you read this book, then I will feel that I have succeeded.

Happy DBAing!

- Mark Sorger

Getting Started with Windows

Why use Windows for Oracle?

Intel-based servers are now moving out of the realm of personal computing and are morphing into industrial-strength servers. The low cost of Intel-based servers is taking the IT industry by storm. With costs as little as one-tenth of proprietary UNIX such as AIX, HP-UX, and Solaris, companies are saving millions of dollars by migrating to Intel platforms.

The only shortcoming of Intel-based servers is their 32-bit architecture. For Oracle, the 32-bit architecture means that very large memory regions (e.g., the Oracle System Global Area) cannot grow beyond four gigabytes – a size far smaller than their 64-bit cousins, where Oracle RAM regions commonly exceed 20 gigabytes.

However, this 32-bit limitation is about to change. The impending availability of Intel 64-bit architecture has caused widespread excitement, and Intel-based servers will soon be able to compete with giant proprietary UNIX servers. IBM has already announced it is abandoning its proprietary AIX UNIX dialect in favor of Linux. While Oracle is quite vocal that Oracle is faster than SQL Server on Intel and has announced a record-breaking benchmark test with the Itanium processors, the company is also very careful not to compare operating system environments.

However, Oracle professionals now have a choice: they can use the Intel-based server on Oracle with Linux or Microsoft Windows. There is a huge debate about which OS is best.

Each Operating system has particular features which might be either an advantage or a disadvantage, depending on the configuration of your Oracle database and the skills of your staff:

Advantages of Oracle UNIX/Linux:

- Significant performance improvement
- Provides high availability
- Contains in-depth system utilities and open-source code
- Highly respected by Oracle personnel

Advantages of Oracle Windows:

- Very easy to deploy and support
- Requires far less IT training
- Simple interface to Microsoft tools such as ODBC and .NET

While opinions vary, here are some specific disadvantages to Linux and Windows:

Disadvantages of Oracle UNIX:

- Requires specialized skills (*vi* editor, shell scripting, etc.)

- Requires highly-technical Systems Administrators and DBAs
- Contains in-depth system utilities and open-source code
- Security holes (if misconfigured)
- Susceptible to root kit attacks

Disadvantages of Oracle Windows:
- Slower than Linux/UNIX
- Less glamorous for the SA and DBA
- History of poor reliability (bad reputation)
- Security holes (if misconfigured)
- Susceptible to Internet viruses

The main disadvantage is regarding the requirements for a technical staff that is proficient in shell scripting, the *vi* editor and the cryptic UNIX command syntax.

Unlike the easy-to-use Windows GUI, Linux and proprietary UNIX often require cryptic shell scripts to perform basic Oracle functions. Given the vast differences in administration, begin with looking at porting from UNIX to Windows.

The core difference is that in UNIX the OS controls the operations, while in Windows the Oracle database controls the operations.

There is also the issue of the expense of licensing the proprietary UNIX software such as Solaris, AIX, and HP UNIX, which can be tens of thousands of dollars. This has led many companies to consider the public-domain Linux option. To understand the benefits and shortcomings of Linux, you must take a closer look at Linux technology.

With the increasing popularity of Intel-based database servers, Oracle shops are struggling to make the choice between Linux and Windows for their Oracle databases. As we may know, Windows has suffered from a history of unreliability and Linux suffers because of its nascent technology and lack of support.

For now, there is no conclusive finding about whether Oracle Intel is best on Linux or Microsoft Windows. Much of the problem lies in the definition of "best." From an Oracle management perspective, Oracle professionals who grew up on the Windows GUI fear having to learn cryptic Linux commands, while UNIX Oracle professionals detest the complicated Windows registry and lack of a command-line interface. From a performance perspective, the debate continues, with neither Linux nor Windows taking a clear lead.

However, one thing is clear: as Intel-based processors leap into a 64-bit architecture, Oracle shops will be rushing to adopt these lower cost server alternatives, and proprietary UNIX vendors such as Hewlett-Packard, Sun, and IBM will also be forced to lower their prices to remain competitive.

Now that we understand the relative advantages on Oracle on Windows, let's take a look at the evolution of Windows to understand the state of Windows technology.

A Brief History of Windows

Before we get into our exploration of managing Oracle on Windows, let's take a trip back in time so that we can put the technology in a historical perspective.

The immediate lineage of Windows Server can be summed up in three letters – VMS. More about that later, but first, for those who want more background, it would seem appropriate to start out with a bit of history on Windows.

In November of 1983, Microsoft Corporation announced Microsoft Windows, a new operating system that provided a then-new idea, graphical user interface, combined with a multitasking environment for computers. Rumor has it that Bill Gates wanted to name the operating system Interface Manager, but his marketing manager convinced him to call it Windows. Microsoft did not actually ship Windows 1.0 until November 20, 1985, almost two years later than the original release date.

Windows started as a desktop product. While working on the Windows product, Bill Gates was also working in conjunction with IBM. Both Gates and IBM were collaborating with each other in developing their PC operating systems and they had to be able to access to each other's code in order to integrate the OS with the hardware.

In August of 1985, the development of OS/2 began when IBM and Microsoft signed the Joint Development Agreement, a joint project aimed at developing and improving the OS/2 operating system.

Windows versus OS/2

By the early 1990s, problems began emerging in Microsoft's relationship with IBM. Microsoft wanted to further develop Windows, while IBM wanted future operating system work to be based on OS/2. In an attempt to resolve the conflict, IBM and Microsoft agreed that IBM would develop OS/2 2.0, to replace OS/2 1.3 and Windows 3.0, while Microsoft would develop a new operating system, OS/2 3.0, to later succeed OS/2 2.0.

Things soon went sour between Gates and IBM, and the Microsoft collaboration with IBM was ended. IBM continued with OS/2, while Microsoft went on to work on "New Technology", or as it is better known, Windows NT.

Although both companies retained the rights to use OS/2 and Windows code developed up to the termination of the agreement, Windows NT was destined to be written almost totally from new roots. Those roots were to come from Digital Equipment Corporation's (DEC) then-flagship operating system.

The Genesis of VMS Affects Windows

Windows NT, (and its descendants Windows 2000/2003/2008), can be traced back in VMS, a favorite O/S of many people who have been in this business for a while. VMS is short for "Virtual Memory System", a multitasking, virtual memory operating system with many users that runs on DEC's Virtual Access Extension (VAE). It is now called OpenVMS.

VMS in its day was used by banks, hospitals, specialty software companies such as Intergraph, and many large businesses. It had a reputation for extreme reliability. It was also the first to use true clusters and actually had a Distributed Lock Manager, allowing several nodes to access the same disk drives at once in much the same way which Oracle RAC functions. That is one thing Microsoft still has not been able to do. Today's Microsoft Clusters can only have one node accessing a disk device at a time.

One of the main architects and project leader of VMS at Digital was Dave Cutler. Once VMS was developed, Dave Cutler and his team continued work on new releases of VMS. By 1981, Cutler was looking to leave Digital. In an attempt to keep him, Digital gave him a new project and about 200 hardware and software engineers with a mission to design a new CPU architecture and OS that would lead Digital into the next decade. The new project was called Prism, and the operating system was slated to be named Mica.

In 1988, Digital cancelled Cutler's project and laid off many of Cutler's group. It was this action that finally caused Cutler to decide to leave Digital, and in August 1988, Bill Gates hired him to work at Microsoft. One of Cutler's conditions for accepting the position at Microsoft was that he could bring several former Digital employees with him, including several hardware engineers. This was agreed upon, the result of which was a team of developers and engineers that had previously built and maintained VMS for several years. These people were the same team that began work on Windows NT at Microsoft.

It would only logically follow that these developers would use their past VMS design experience directly in the design and implementation of NT. Many users believe that NT's developers carried concepts from VMS to NT, but most do not know just how similar NT and VMS actually are at the kernel level. The result is, if a DBA has worked with VMS, Windows NT/Server 200x really is not as much of a shock as it is to someone who is coming over from UNIX/Linux.

Now that we understand how Windows has its roots in VMS, let's take a closer look at the threaded model on Windows.

The Threaded Model on Windows

One of the things to get used to with Oracle on Windows versus other operating systems such as UNIX or Linux is that instead of using a process-based server, Windows uses a thread-based server. Using Oracle to illustrate, on operating systems such as UNIX or Linux, Oracle uses separate processes to run all the background tasks, i.e. PMON, SMON, LGWR, and such. In addition, each new database connection spawns yet another UNIX/Linux process.

On UNIX, there are separate background processes:

```
>ps -ef | grep ora_

oracle 23549    1    0    Jan 12 ?          0:09 ora_qmnc_orcl
oracle 23514    1    0    Jan 12 ?          1:36 ora_pmon_orcl
oracle 23528    1    0    Jan 12 ?          0:00 ora_reco_orcl
oracle 23532    1    0    Jan 12 ?          0:38 ora_mmon_orcl
oracle 23524    1    0    Jan 12 ?          1:53 ora_ckpt_orcl
oracle 23522    1    0    Jan 12 ?          1:38 ora_lgwr_orcl
oracle 23534    1    0    Jan 12 ?          2:37 ora_mmnl_orcl
oracle 23547    1    0    Jan 12 ?          0:07 ora_arc1_orcl
oracle 23518    1    0    Jan 12 ?          0:07 ora_mman_orcl
oracle 23516    1    0    Jan 12 ?          0:09 ora_psp0_orcl
oracle 23545    1    0    Jan 12 ?          0:14 ora_arc0_orcl
```

```
root 23541      1    0    Jan 12 ?        0:01 ora_dism_orcl
oracle 23520    1    0    Jan 12 ?        0:38 ora_dbw0_orcl
oracle 23526    1    0    Jan 12 ?        1:30 ora_smon_orcl
```

With Windows, there are processes which are defined as executing programs. However, with Windows there are also one or more threads running in the context of each process.

As in UNIX/Linux, there are PMON, SMON, LGWR, and such running on Windows supporting the Oracle instance. However, in Windows, all of these are implemented as threads inside one single process called *oracle.exe*. These threads all run inside this single Windows process.

Not only do all the database support threads run under this one process, but so do all of the user connections, unlike UNIX/Linux where a new operating system process is seen for each new Oracle connection. In Windows, all that shows in the Task Manager is *oracle.exe* – everything related to that Oracle instance is running as Windows threads inside that process. There is one *oracle.exe* process for each Oracle instance that is running on the server. So, the ability to control Oracle user processes at the Operating System level is lost. It is not possible to kill any errant user processes with a *kill -9* like you can in UNIX.

Items such as the Oracle listener, Oracle Grid Control Agent, and more can also be seen as separate Windows processes in the Task Manager. If there are multiple Oracle listeners, each will have its own process. Each will also have a Windows service associated with it, but that will be covered in a later chapter.

Now that we understand the major differences between Windows and other operating systems, let's take a look at how to choose the best release of Windows and Oracle.

Choosing the Best Release of Windows and Oracle

A top-down approach is best for choosing the right version of Windows for the application, especially if the application will be running on the same server as the database. Start with the requirements of the Application software that will be used on the system, then consider the requirements of the version of Oracle supported by that application. Generally, software vendors certify their software with certain releases of Oracle, so be sure to check. Other combinations may work, but may not be supported by the Application Software Vendor.

> ⌸ **User ID = book, Password = reader**

Windows: Standard or Enterprise?

Oracle 11g currently supports Windows 2003 and Windows 2008 Enterprise and Standard editions, both 32 and 64 bit. Whichever one is chosen, it makes sense to patch it to the latest Service Pack prior to using it.

The most compelling reason to use Windows Enterprise Edition over Standard in the context of Oracle would be the ability to use Microsoft Clusters. The only reason to use that would be if Oracle Failsafe needs to be used, a Windows-only feature of Oracle that allows active-passive failover. Microsoft Clustering is an entire subject by itself, and will not be covered here.

Windows: 32- or 64-Bit?

The difference between 32-bit and 64-bit Windows is obviously address space. Mathematically, there is only 4 GB of available memory address space on a 32-bit server. Windows by default separates this out into 2 GB for user process and 2 GB for operating system tasks.

What this means to the Oracle DBA is that there is a limit of 2 GB for the SGA and all the other Oracle support jobs and user jobs for an

---

Oracle instance. (Remember the threaded model covered earlier). In actual practice, once this gets over about 1.7GB, the limit is being met. This means in Oracle 11gR2, there cannot be a MEMORY_TARGET over 1.7GB, and in prior releases, SGA and PGA together should not exceed 1.7GB.

If this is not evident on a 32-bit Oracle Windows Server and an attempt is made to increase the SGA beyond 2 GB, *ORA-27102* out of memory errors will appear when the database is restarted.

```
C:\>sqlplus "/ as sysdba"
```

```
SQL*Plus: Release 10.2.0.4.0 - Production on Sat Apr 25 15:57:04 2009
Copyright (c) 1982, 2007, Oracle.  All Rights Reserved.
Connected to an idle instance.
SQL>
startup
ORA-27102: out of memory
OSD-00029: additional error information
O/S-Error: (OS 8) Not enough storage is available to process this command.
SQL>
exit
C:>
```

One remedy to this is to set the /3 GB switch in the *boot.ini* file on the server. This activates a Windows feature called 4 GB RAM Tuning (4GT). This feature causes Windows to reallocate an extra 1 GB of memory for the application process, causing the split to now be 3GB for application use and 1GB for operating system use.

This is done as follows:

1. Make a copy of *C:\boot.ini*

2. Edit *C:\boot.ini*

3. Add /3 GB to the end of the boot string

4. Reboot the server

Example:

```
[boot loader]
```

```
timeout=30
default=multi(0)disk(0)rdisk(0)partition(1)\WINDOWS
[operating systems]
multi(0)disk(0)rdisk(0)partition(1)\WINDOWS="Windows Server 2003, Enterprise"
/noexecute=optout /fastdetect /3GB
```

This can be tweaked a bit by including the /USERVA switch along with the /3 GB switch. What this does is allow for modifying how much of the OS memory can actually be allocated for processes. For example, /USERVA=2800 will give 2.8GB for processes and 1.2GB for the OS, giving a bit more for paged pool and such.

Beware of one thing here: if the /3 GB switch is set and an attempt is made to copy large files, "not enough resources" errors may occur. This is due to a lack of paged memory since half of it was stolen from the OS!

In Windows 2008, there is no longer a *boot.ini* file. However, the same result can be accomplished using *bcdedit.exe*. It also does many other things, but this will just review setting /3 GB. The command from the command prompt is:

```
bcdedit /set increaseuserva 3072
```

3072 is the number of megabytes that a user-mode process can use. So, to allow 3GB of memory, 3*1024 MB = 3072 MB is used. This can be set as needed, the same as using /3 GB and /USERVA in the *boot.ini* for Windows 2003. To set /3 GB /USERVA=2800, the command would be:

```
bcdedit /set increaseuserva 2800.
```

Another solution to squeeze more memory for Oracle out of a 32-bit system is to use Oracle AWE (Address Windowing Extensions) to get even more memory. Information on this can be found in Metalink Note 225349.1.

The bottom line is that using 64-bit Windows if given a choice is the best bet. That way, the memory addressing becomes a non-issue.

Commonly Used Windows Commands

Windows is far and away a GUI (Graphical User Interface) driven operating system, and many users never even use the command prompt. However, as an Oracle DBA it is quite useful to be able to operate at the command prompt level. Once you have an understanding of the basic commands, they can be used for many things that are not possible from a GUI, and can also be used in scripts.

This section will briefly review commonly used Windows commands, and if needed, the user can delve deeper and study them in further detail. At times, the related UNIX/Linux command will be given.

This is to give readers from a UNIX/Linux background a starting point for understanding them. These commands, as will be seen in later chapters, allow some scripting to be done as well as be operated at the command prompt. Network related commands are covered in Chapter 8.

```
'help' first! :
```

First and foremost, to get help on any command, at the command prompt type the command, followed by the /? or *help* command. The *help* command by itself will list all the available O/S commands. Remember Windows is not case sensitive, so upper, lower, or mixed case can be used and it will not matter.

Example:

```
C:\Documents and Settings>help dir

Displays a list of files and subdirectories in a directory.

DIR [drive:][path][filename] [/A[[:]attributes]] [/B] [/C] [/D] [/L] [/N]
```

```
   [/O[[:]sortorder]] [/P] [/Q] [/S] [/T[[:]timefield]] [/W] [/X] [/4]
```

[drive:][path][filename]: Specifies drive, directory, and/or files to list.

```
/A          Displays files with specified attributes.
            attributes
               D  Directories      R  Read-only files
               H  Hidden files     A  Files ready for archiving
               S  System files -   Prefix meaning not
/B          Uses bare format (no heading information or
            summary).
/C          Display the thousand separator in file sizes.
            This is the default.  Use /-C to disable
            display of separator.
/D          Same as wide but files are list sorted by
            column.
/L          Uses lowercase.
/N          New long list format where filenames are on
            the far right.
/O          List by files in sorted order.
            sortorder
               N  By name (alphabetic)     S  By size (smallest first)
               E  By extension (alphabetic) D  By date/time (oldest first)
               G  Group directories first   -  Prefix to reverse order
/P          Pauses after each full screen of information.
/Q          Display the owner of the file.
/S          Displays files in specified directory and all subdirectories.
/T          Controls which time field displayed or used for sorting timefield
               C  Creation
               A  Last Access
               W  Last Written
/ W         Uses wide list format.
  X         This displays the short names generated for non-8dot3 file names.
            The format is that of /N with the short name inserted before the
            long name. If no short name is present, blanks are displayed in its place.
/4          Displays four-digit years
```

Switches may be preset in the *dircmd* environment variable. Override preset switches by prefixing any switch with - (hyphen); for example, */-W*.

Typing *help* at the command prompt will give a summary list of all the commands:

```
C:\Documents and Settings> help
```

For more information on a specific command, type *help command-name*:

```
ASSOC    Displays or modifies file extension associations
AT       Schedules commands and programs to run on a
         computer
ATTRIB   Displays or changes file attributes
BREAK    Sets or clears extended CTRL+C checking
CACLS    Displays or modifies access control lists (ACLs) of
         files
CALL     Calls one batch program from another
CD       Displays the name of or changes the current
```

```
            directory
CHCP       Displays or sets the active code page number
CHDIR      Displays the name of or changes the current
            directory
CHKDSK     Checks a disk and displays a status report
CHKNTFS    Displays or modifies the checking of disk at boot
            time
CLS        Clears the screen
CMD        Starts a new instance of the Windows command
            interpreter
COLOR      Sets the default console foreground and background
            colors
COMP       Compares the contents of two files or sets of
            files
COMPACT    Displays or alters the compression of files on NTFS
            partitions
CONVERT    Converts FAT volumes to NTFS.  You cannot convert
            the current drive.
COPY       Copies one or more files to another location
DATE       Displays or sets the date
DEL        Deletes one or more files
DIR        Displays a list of files and subdirectories in a
            directory
DISKCOMP   Compares the contents of two floppy disks
DISKCOPY   Copies the contents of one floppy disk to another
DOSKEY     Edits command lines, recalls Windows commands, and
            creates macros
ECHO       Displays messages, or turns command echoing on or
            off
ENDLOCAL   Ends localization of environment changes in a batch
            file
ERASE      Deletes one or more files
EXIT       Quits the cmd.exe program (command interpreter)
FC         Compares two files or sets of files, and displays
            the differences between them
FIND       Searches for a text string in a file or files
FINDSTR    Searches for strings in files
FOR        Runs a specified command for each file in a set of
            files
FORMAT     Formats a disk for use with Windows
FTYPE      Displays or modifies file types used in file
            extension associations
GOTO       Directs the Windows command interpreter to a
            labeled line in a batch program
GRAFTABL   Enables Windows to display an extended character
            set in graphics mode
HELP       Provides Help information for Windows commands
IF         Performs conditional processing in batch programs
LABEL      Creates, changes, or deletes the volume label of a
            disk
MD         Creates a directory
MKDIR      Creates a directory
MODE       Configures a system device
MORE       Displays output one screen at a time
MOVE       Moves one or more files from one directory to
            another directory
PATH       Displays or sets a search path for executable
            files
PAUSE      Suspends processing of a batch file and displays a
```

```
              message
POPD          Restores the previous value of the current
              directory saved by PUSHD
PRINT         Prints a text file
PROMPT        Changes the Windows command prompt
PUSHD         Saves the current directory then changes it
RD            Removes a directory
RECOVER       Recovers readable information from a bad or
              defective disk
REM           Records comments (remarks) in batch files or
              config.sys
REN           Renames a file or files
RENAME        Renames a file or files
REPLACE       Replaces files
RMDIR         Removes a directory
SET           Displays, sets, or removes Windows environment variables.
SETLOCAL      Begins localization of environment changes in a
              batch file
SHIFT         Shifts the position of replaceable parameters in
              batch files
SORT          Sorts input
START         Starts a separate window to run a specified program
              or command
SUBST         Associates a path with a drive letter
TIME          Displays or sets the system time
TITLE         Sets the window title for a cmd.exe session
TREE          Graphically displays the directory structure of a
              drive or path
TYPE          Displays the contents of a text file
VER           Displays the Windows version
VERIFY        Tells Windows whether to verify that your files are
              written correctly to a disk
VOL           Displays a disk volume label and serial number
XCOPY         Copies files and directory trees

C:\Documents and Settings>
```

Next we will review some common UNIX commands and their Windows counterparts.

UNIX Versus DOS Commands

Back in the days before Microsoft Windows dominated the PC market, operating systems were controlled by commands. PC users were required to learn these commands in order to perform tasks. During the 1980s, Microsoft DOS dominated the PC market while the early UNIX command systems were used on larger multi-processing servers. The main difference between UNIX and DOS is that DOS was originally designed for single-user systems, while UNIX was designed for systems with many users.

While PC's have evolved into GUI interfaces such as Windows, UNIX systems have never evolved into GUI environments. Hence, The Oracle professional must master a bewildering number of cryptic UNIX commands in order to manage their Oracle databases.

One of the most confounding issues for the UNIX beginner is being confronted with a complex UNIX command. The cryptic nature of UNIX is such that even the most seasoned UNIX professional may have trouble deciphering the purpose of the command.

However, because UNIX and MS-DOS were developed at the same time, they share some common syntax. Here are some things that work the same way in MS-DOS as in UNIX:

- *ping*
- *netstat*
- *ftp*
- *more*
- *mkdir*
- *nslookup*

Of course many commands are different between UNIX and MS-DOS. Below is a simple table showing some common UNIX commands and their Windows counterparts.

UNIX/Linux	MS-DOS	Command Function
--	cd -	Switch between current and last directory
cat	Type	Displays the contents of a file
cd	Cd	Moves from one directory to another
cd /u01/test	cd c:\u01\test	Change directory paths
cd ..	cd..	Go up in directory
chmod	Attrib	Sets file permissions
clear	Cls	Clear the screen

UNIX/Linux	MS-DOS	Command Function
cp	copy	Copies a file (or a group of files)
diff	fc	Compare two files
cpio	xcopy	Backs up and recovers files
date	date	Display the system date
doskey	\<ctl> k (3)	Display command history
export PS1='xx'	prompt	Change the command prompt text
find	grep	Find a character string in a file
gzip	dblspace	Compress a data file
ln	--	Forms a link to a file
lp	print	Queues a file for printing
lpstat	print	Displays the printing queue
ls -al	dir	Displays the contents of a directory
mem	lsdev (2)	Display RAM memory
mkdir	md	Creates a new subdirectory
move	cp (4)	Move a file to another directory
mv	rename	Renames a file
rm	del	Deletes a file (or group of files)
rmdir	rd	Deletes an existing directory
setenv (1)	set	Set an environment variable
sort	sort	Sorts lines in a file
ver	uname -a	Display OS version
vi	edit	Creates and edits text

Now that we have covered some MS-DOS commands and their functions, let's look at commands used specifically with the directory.

Directory Commands

Out of the list of all O/S commands, there are several commands specifically geared towards working with the directory:

- *cd:* This is the same as the UNIX/Linux *cd*. It changes the current working directory to whatever path that is entered. The syntax is:

```
cd   C:\oracle\10.2.0.4\network\admin
```

There is a twist, however. If the directory that needs to be changed is on a different drive, specify that drive first, then type the *cd* command; otherwise, Windows will not be able to find the directory. Providing a full path including the drive letter still will not work unless the following is done first:

```
C:\>  D:

D:\>  cd d:\newdir

D:\newdir>
```

- *dir:* Simply put, this gives a directory listing of the current working directory. By adding a path, it will give a directory of that folder.

Example:

```
C:\> dir

C:\> dir C:\oracle\product\10.2.0\client_1\network\admin
```

There are many switches available, but we will touch on the ones we find most useful.

```
/B         Uses bare format (no heading information or summary).
/O         List by files in sorted order.
           sortorder
           N  By name (alphabetic)      S  By size (smallest first)
           E  By extension (alphabetic)  D  By date/time (oldest first)
           G  Group directories first  -  Prefix to reverse order
/P         Pauses after each screenful of information.
/S         Displays files in specified directory and all subdirectories.
```

Switches can be reset in the *dircmd* environment variable. Override preset switches by prefixing any switch with - (hyphen); for example, /-W.

```
C:\Documents and Settings\Mill>
```

- *mkdir:* This is used to create a directory. In Windows, they are called folders or subfolders. All that needs to be done is either *cd* to the top level and *mkdir* the subdirectory, or specify a full path. All upper level directories must exist before the lowest level can be created.

For example:

```
mkdir D:\oracle\oradata\sid_one\dbf would only work if
D:\oracle\oradata\sid_one already existed.
```

Alternately, it could be scripted as:

```
mkdir D:\oracle
mkdir D:\oracle\oradata
mkdir D:\oracle\oradata\sid_one
mkdir D:\oracle\oradata\sid_one\dbf
```

- *rmdir*: This deletes a directory. Generally, it makes sense to delete all the files underneath first, but the */s* switch can also be used to delete the directory and everything under it. The */q* switch disables prompts asking if it is OK to delete.

Example:

```
rmdir /S  /Q  D:\oracle\oradata\sid_one
```

This would delete all files and subfolders under and including:

```
D:\oracle\oradata\sid_one
```

Be careful with this one!

Now that we see how directory commands work, let's look at some common Windows file commands.

Windows File Commands

The following are commands that are used to find information about files.

- *type*: This is similar to the UNIX/Linux command *cat*. It does what the name implies, namely typing out the contents of a file. The syntax is:

```
TYPE [drive:] [path] filename
```

An example would be:

```
C:\Oracle\product\10.2.0.4\network\admin>  type listener.ora
```

- *more*: This command is similar to *type*, except that it stops at each full screen instead of continuously scrolling past. The UNIX/Linux command *more* works the same way. Typing *return* displays the next line of text, and typing *space* displays the next full screen.

```
C:\>  more initORCL.ora
```

The *more* command can also be used with a pipe, like in UNIX, to display the output of a Windows command screen by screen. For example:

```
C:\> dir | more
```

- *del*: This deletes a file or files. The */Q*, meaning quiet, switch disables the prompts asking if it is OK to delete.

Example:

```
del /Q  D:\oracle\oradata\orcl\exports\export.dmp
```

This would delete the single file:

```
D:\oracle\oradata\orcl\exports\export.dmp without any prompts.
```

- *copy*: This copies a file or files to a new destination. The /Y switch suppresses all verification prompts, again useful in scripts.

```
COPY [/D] [/V] [/N] [/Y | /-Y] [/Z] [/A | /B ] source [/A | /B]
     [+ source [/A | /B] [+ ...]] [destination [/A | /B]]
```

source	Specifies the file or files to be copied.
/A	Indicates an ASCII text file.
/B	Indicates a binary file.
/D	Allow the destination file to be created at a decrypted destination. Specifies the directory and/or filename for the new files(s).
/V	Verifies that new files are written correctly.
/N	Uses short filename, if available, when copying a file with a non-8dot3 name.
/Y	Suppresses prompting to confirm you want to overwrite an existing destination file.
/-Y	Causes prompting to confirm you want to overwrite an existing destination file.
/Z	Copies networked files in restartable mode.

The switch /Y may be preset in the *copycmd* environment variable. This can be overridden with /-Y on the command line. Default is to prompt on overwrites unless the *copy* command is being executed from within a batch script.

To append files, specify a single file for destination but multiple files for source using wildcards or file1+file2+file3 format.

- *xcopy*: This works the same as *copy* except it allows moving entire directory trees, while *copy* only moves individual files. This allows keeping a directory structure intact on the copy, and is useful for things such as copying Oracle database files for cold saves.

```
XCOPY source [destination] [/A | /M] [/D[:date]] [/P] [/S [/E]] [/V] [/W]
                           [/C] [/I] [/Q] [/F] [/L] [/G] [/H] [/R] [/T] [/U]
                           [/K] [/N] [/O] [/X] [/Y] [/-Y] [/Z]
                           [/EXCLUDE:file1[+file2][+file3]...]
```

source	Specifies the file(s) to copy
destination	Specifies the location and/or name of new files
/A	Copies only files with the archive attribute

	set; does not change the attribute.

/M   Copies only files with the archive attribute
            set; turns off the archive attribute.

/D:m-d-y   Copies files changed on or after the specified date.

            If no date is given, copies only those files whose

            source time is newer than the destination time.

/EXCLUDE: file1[+file2][+file3]... Specifies a list of files
            containing strings. Each string should be in a
            separate line in the files. When any of the strings
            match any part of the absolute path of the file to be
            copied, that file will be excluded from being copied.
            For example, specifying a string like \obj\ or .obj
            will exclude all files underneath the directory obj
            or all files with the .obj extension, respectively.

/P   Prompts before creating each destination file

/S   Copies directories and subdirectories except empty
            ones

/E   Copies directories and subdirectories, including
            empty ones. Same as /S /E. May be used to modify /T

/V   Verifies each new file

/W   Prompts pressing a key before copying

/C   Continues copying even if errors occur

/I   If destination does not exist and copying more than
            one file, assumes that destination must be a

            directory.

/Q   Does not display file names while copying

/F   Displays full source and destination file names while
            copying

/L   Displays files that would be copied

/G   Allows the copying of encrypted files to destination
            that does not support encryption

/H   Copies hidden and system files also

/R   Overwrites read-only files

/T   Creates directory structure, but does not copy files
            Does not include empty directories or subdirectories.
            /T /E includes empty directories and subdirectories.

/U   Copies only files that already exist in destination

```
/K              Copies attributes. Normal Xcopy will reset read-only
                attributes.
/N              Copies using the generated short names

/O              Copies file ownership and ACL information

/X              Copies file audit settings (implies /O)

/Y              Suppresses prompting to confirm you want to overwrite

                an existing destination file
/-Y             Causes prompting to confirm you want to overwrite an
                existing destination file

/Z              Copies networked files in restartable mode
```

The switch /Y may be preset in the *copycmd* environment variable. This may be overridden with /-Y on the command line.

As we can see, these file commands can be quite useful. Now let's move on to cover the *find* and *findstr* commands, which can be used to perform string searches in Windows.

String Searches in Windows

There are two different commands to search for text. The *find* command is very basic and searches for a single string in a file and returns the resultant line. The other is far more powerful: *findstr*. This command searches for a single string, multiple strings, or an exact phrase:

- *findstr* "abc" finds the string "abc"

- *findstr* "abc 123" finds "abc" OR "123"

- *findstr* /C:"abc 123" finds "abc 123"

Both the *find* and *findstr* commands will be demonstrated next.

Using the find Command

```
find [/V] [/C] [/N] [/I] [/OFF[LINE]] "string" [[drive:][path]filename[
...]]
```

```
/V      Displays all lines NOT containing the specified string

/C      Displays only the count of lines containing the string

/N      Displays line numbers with the displayed lines

/I      Ignores the case of characters when searching for the string

/OFF[LINE]  Do not skip files with offline attribute set
"string"     Specifies the text string to find
[drive:][path]filename  Specifies a file or files to search
```

If a path is not specified, *find* searches the text typed at the prompt or piped from another command.

Using the findstr Command

```
FINDSTR [/B] [/E] [/L] [/R] [/S] [/I] [/X] [/V] [/N] [/M] [/O] [/P]
[/F:file]
       [/C:string] [/G:file] [/D:dir list] [/A:color attributes]
[/OFF[LINE]]
       strings [[drive:][path]filename[ ...]]
```

```
/B      Matches pattern if at the beginning of a line

/E      Matches pattern if at the end of a line

/L      Uses search strings literally

/R      Uses search strings as regular expressions

/S      Searches for matching files in the current directory and all
        subdirectories

/I      Specifies that the search is not to be case-sensitive

/X      Prints lines that match exactly

/V      Prints only lines that do not contain a match

/N      Prints the line number before each line that matches

/M      Prints only the filename if a file contains a match

/O      Prints character offset before each matching line

/P      Skip files with non-printable characters

/OFF[LINE]  Do not skip files with offline attribute set

/A:attr     Specifies color attribute with two hex digits. See "color /?"
/F:file     Reads file list from the specified file (/ stands for console)
```

```
/C:string  Uses specified string as a literal search string

/G:file    Gets search strings from the specified file (/ stands for
console)
/D:dir     Search a semicolon delimited list of directories
strings    Text to be searched for
[drive:][path]filename  Specifies a file or files to search.

Use spaces to separate multiple search strings unless the argument is
prefixed with /C   For example, 'findstr "hello there" x.y' searches for
"hello" or "there" in file x.y.   'findstr /C:"hello there" x.y' searches for
"hello there" in file x.y.
```

Below is a quick reference of regular expressions (regex) for *find*:

- Wildcard: Any character
- *: Repeat; zero or more occurrences of previous character or class
- ^: Line position; beginning of line
- $: Line position; end of line
- [class]: Character class; any one character in set
- [^class]: Inverse class; any one character not in set
- [x-y]: Range; any characters within the specified range
- \x: Escape; literal use of metacharacter x
- \<xyz: Word position; beginning of word
- xyz\>: Word position; end of word

For full information on *findstr* regular expressions, refer to the online Command Reference.

The final section of this chapter will provide a brief overview of Windows executables.

Windows Executables

The following table lists the Windows executables provided by Oracle. Many of the utilities provided in UNIX are also available in Windows. This list has been restricted to those utilities that are only present on the Windows platform.

Executable	Description	First Available
dbsnmp.exe	Intelligent Agent	8.1.5
dbsnmpj.exe	Intelligent Agent Job Processor (nothing to do with Java or JRE)	8.1.5
encaps.exe	SNMP encapsulation agent	Default in 9.0.1 Custom in 8i and below
encsvc.exe	SNMP encapsulation service	Default in 9.0.1 Custom in 8i and below
launch.exe	Java code launcher	8.0
launchem.exe	Enterprise Manager Launcher	8.0
ocopy.exe	File copy utility	(7.3.4)
OMSNTsrv.exe	Oracle Management Server	9.2.0
omtsreco.exe	MTS Recovery	9.0.1
OO4OCODEWIZ.EXE	Oracle Objects for OLE Code Wizard	9.2.0
OracleAdNetConnect.exe	MFC Application	8.1.7
OracleAdNetTest.exe	MFC Application	9.0.1
oradim.exe	Manages oracle instances	(7.3.4)
orakill.exe	Process killer	(7.3.4)
oramts_deinst.exe	Unknown	9.2.0
Orastack.exe	Modifies stack RAM	(7.3.4)
Pagntsrv.exe	OEM Paging Server	9.0.1
tdvapp.exe	Trace Data Viewer	9.0.1
Selecthome.bat	Change oracle home	10gR2
Isqlpussvc	Isqlplus service startup	10gR2
VDOShell.exe	Oracle Expert	9.0.1
vmq.exe	SQL Analyze	9.0.1
Vtushell.exe	OEM Index Tuning Wizard	9.0.1
xpautune.exe	Oracle Expert	9.0.1
xpcoin.exe	Oracle Expert	9.0.1
xpksh.exe	Oracle Expert Command Shell	9.0.1
xpui.exe	Oracle Expert	9.0.1

Summary

This chapter has provided a brief history of Windows and some common Windows commands and executables. Of course there are many other Windows commands that can be used, but the above are the most common. The best way to really learn how these and others work is to go and try them to see what they do! Quite a bit can be learned that way.

The main points of this chapter include:

- Windows has a stormy history
- How VMS affected Windows
- Choosing the best release of Windows and Oracle
- Commonly used Windows commands
- UNIX versus DOS commands
- String Searches in Windows
- Windows executables

The next chapter involves working with users and groups, including adding new ones.

Windows User and Group Management

Introduction

Windows uses users and groups much the same as in any other operating system. There are users and groups on the local system, as well as users and groups that can be maintained on the enterprise-wide level using the Windows Active Directory. The Active Directory is a detailed subject in itself, so only users and groups on the local system will be reviewed here.

If the user is on an Active Directory network, local rights on the server will still be needed as well as being a member of the local ORA_DBA group on the server in order to do things such as *connect / as sysdba*.

This chapter will begin with a brief overview of users and groups, and will then demonstrate how to add users, how to add groups, and how to add users to groups.

About Users and Groups

The "oracle" user ID and the proper group are important to the management of the Oracle database because there must be a single user account that manages and controls the Oracle database interface with Windows.

This "master" Windows has the privileges governed by the Windows group, and it is this group (named like dba or ora_dba), which is granted to the Windows user in order to give this user the privileges necessary to execute the programs within the $ORACLE_HOME/bin directory.

These "external" Windows executable programs include:

- *sqlplus* as SYSDBA: To startup & shutdown the database
- *lsnrctl:* To manage the listener process
- *expdp:* To invoke a database export
- *impdp:* To invoke a database import
- *dbverify:* To verify database integrity
- *asmcmd:* Manage ASM data files
- *adrci:* Automatic diagnostic repository commands

The following sections will demonstrate how to define the Oracle database user, how to define the Oracle database group, and how to assign the user to your Oracle DBA group. You will then be able to execute these native utilities from the DOS command line prompt.

The Computer Management Screen

In order to work with local users and groups, we must first go to the *Computer Management* screen. This looks a bit different on Windows 2008 than on Windows 2003, but the functionality is similar. The easiest way to get there on both is to click the *Start* button on the bottom left of the taskbar, right click on *My Computer*, and then select *Manage* as seen in Figure 2.1.

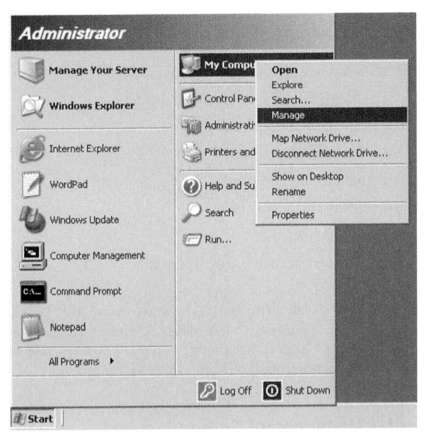

Figure 2.1: *Manage Computer Option*

When *Manage* is clicked, the *Computer Management* screen appears like in Figure 2.2.

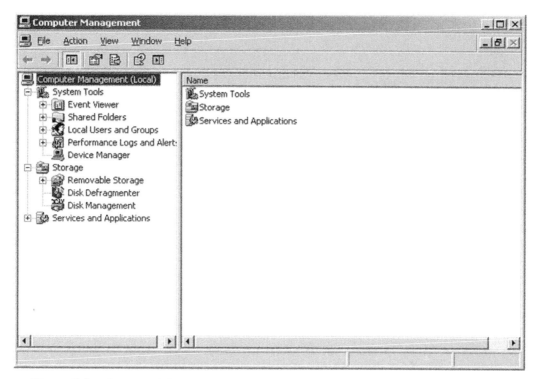

Figure 2.2: *Computer Management Screen*

Next to be examined is how to work with users and groups using this screen.

Working with Users and Groups

Now that the Computer Management screen is active, it is a simple matter to navigate to the *Users and Groups* selection. Simply move the mouse over the + sign next to *Users and Groups*, or mouse over the text and click. Using the + sign will expand the selection into *Users* and *Groups* folders directly underneath, as shown in Figure 2.3. Clicking on the text will display the same folders, but it will appear in the right hand pane instead, as seen in Figure 2.4.

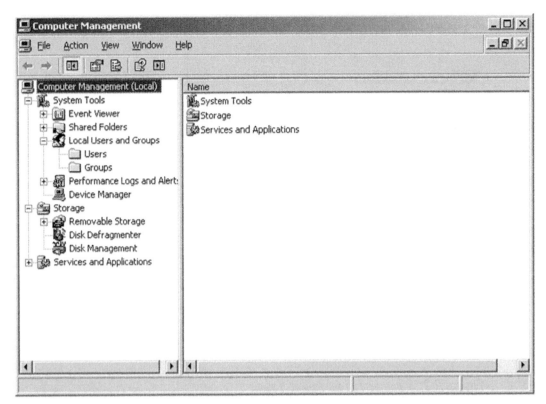

Figure 2.3: *Navigating to Users and Groups Selection*

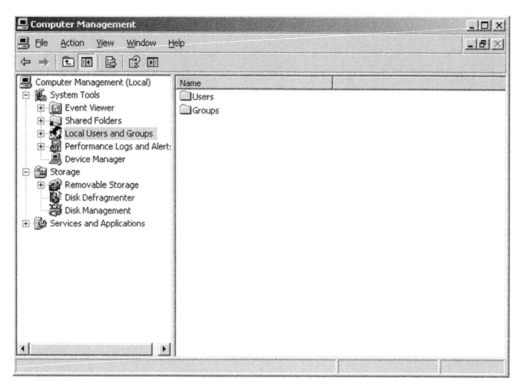

Figure 2.4: *Users and Groups Screen*

Clicking on the *Users* folder displays the user accounts on the local server, as seen in the next figure (Figure 2.5).

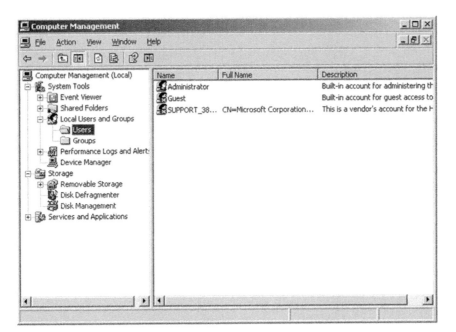

Figure 2.5: *User Accounts Screen*

Clicking on *Groups* shows all of the groups on the local server (Figure 2.6).

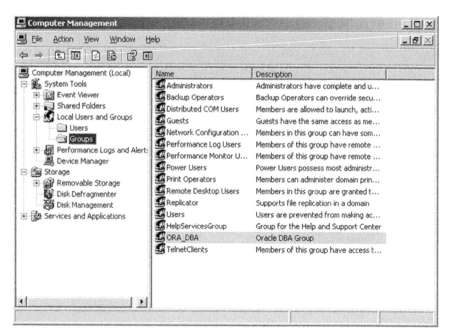

Figure 2.6: *Groups Listing Screen*

Now that we have covered how to get to the screen for managing users and groups, we will examine how to add a user.

Adding a User

Generally, it is recommended to install and run Oracle from a user account other than the server Administrator account. Permissions can be granted to the new user, and it can be added to the appropriate groups such as Administrator and ORA_DBA.

In order to create a user, mouse over the *Users* folder, right click and select *New User* as shown in Figure 2.7.

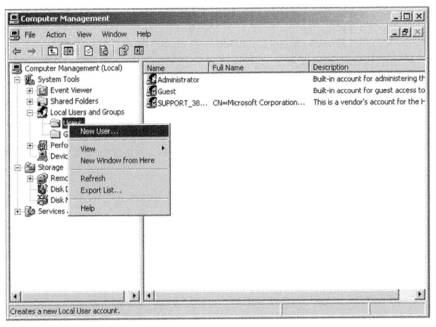

Figure 2.7: *New User Screen*

Once *New User* has been clicked, the *Add User* screen appears and the user name and other information can be inserted, as seen in the following screen (Figure 2.8). After all information has been entered, click *Create* at the bottom of the screen to create the user account.

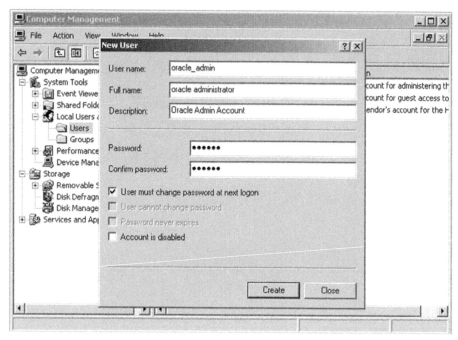

Figure 2.8: *Add User Screen*

Now that adding a user has been demonstrated, we will move on to discuss adding a group.

Adding a Group

In order to create a group, mouse over the *Groups* folder, right click and select *New Group* as shown in Figure 2.9.

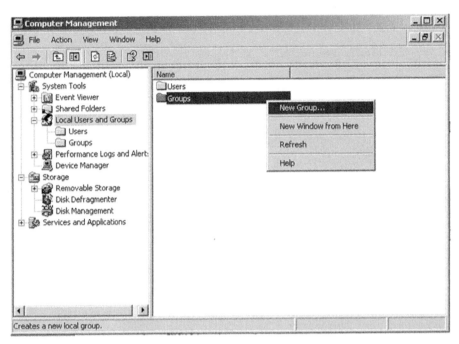

Figure 2.9: *Select New Group*

The *New Group* screen appears. Use this screen to enter the group name and description, and then click the *Create* button as shown in Figure 2.10.

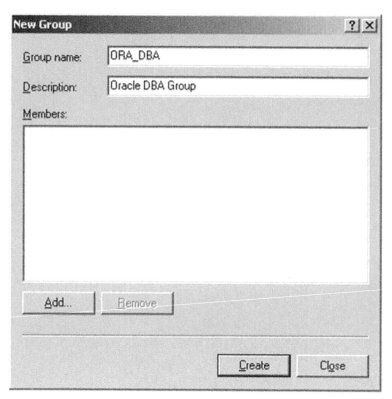

Figure 2.10: *Name Group Screen*

Clicking *Create* will go back to an empty *New Group* screen as seen in Figure 2.11, but the group has been created. Click *Close* to exit.

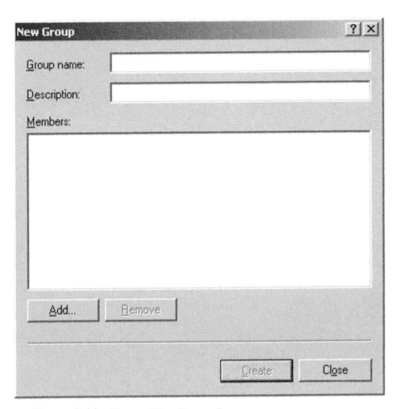

Figure 2.11: *Empty New Group Screen*

Now that we have covered creating a new user and a new group, we will now examine how to add a user to a group.

Adding a User to a Group

Now that the *oracle_admin* user and ORA_DBA group have been created, it is time to add the *oracle_admin* user to the ORA_DBA group.

This is done as follows: First, click on the *Groups* folder in Computer Management, right click on the ORA_DBA group in the right hand pane, and select *Add to Group* (Figure 2.12).

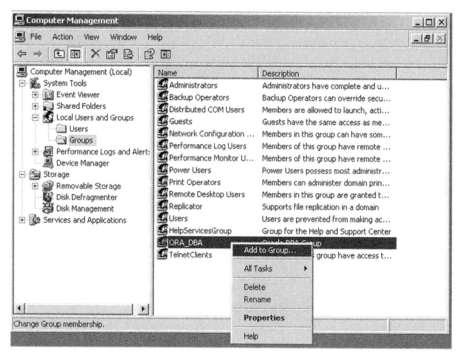

Figure 2.12: *Add to Group Screen*

This screen displays the group properties, listing all current members of the group (Figure 2.13).

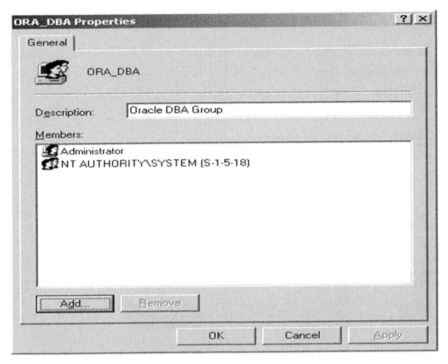

Figure 2.13: *Group Properties Screen*

Click *Add* to get to the *Select Users* screen.

On the *Select Users* screen, type in the user name to be added. In this example, it is *oracle_admin* as shown in Figure 2.14.

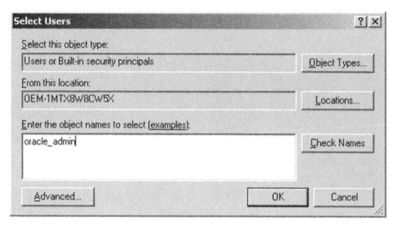

Figure 2.14: *Name Users Screen*

To verify that this is a valid choice, click the *Check Names* button. This returns validation, after which *OK* can be selected as seen in the next screen.

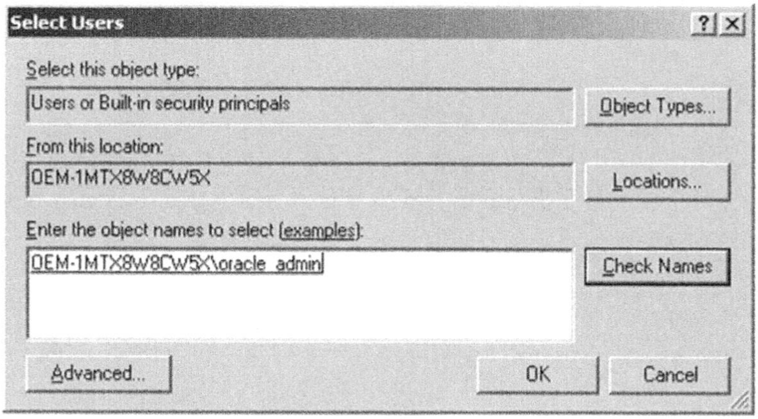

Figure 2.15: *Check Names Screen*

Oracle_admin has now been added as a member of the ORA_DBA group. Several options are now available. To apply and exit, select *OK*. To add the member but remain in the screen, select *Apply*. To exit without adding the user, select *Cancel*.

Figure 2.16: *Group Members*

Conclusion

Working with local users and groups was the focus of this chapter. By using the *Computer Management* screen, it was shown, step-by-step, how to go about adding a user, adding a group, and adding a user to a group.

Now that we have covered the basics of managing users and groups, let's move on to examine the Windows Task Manager and Performance Monitor.

Windows Performance Monitoring and the Event Viewer

Introduction

Windows provides many tools for performance monitoring and viewing system logs. The Windows Performance Monitor and Windows Task Manager are used for monitoring whatever could possibly be needed on the server, and the Windows Event Viewer allows the DBA to look at System, Security, and Application logs. These logs are useful for determining the cause of failures, security related items, and even Oracle related items.

The following topics will be covered in this chapter:

- Windows Task Manager
- Windows Performance Monitor
- Saving settings to a file
- Saving sessions to a logfile
- Playing back monitor sessions
- Windows Event Viewer (Windows 2003 and 2008)
- Saving to a CSV or other file type

We will begin by taking a look at the Windows Task Manager.

Windows Task Manager

The Windows Task Manager is a very quick and handy tool for seeing what is going on with the server. The Task Manager shows memory usa

list   The process

the   ɔnes are using

alp   so be sorted

heɛ   llowing many

Th   ck the task bar

anɑ   *l-Alt-Delete* and

selɛ   k Manager can

dis   ɪg), Processes

(pɛ   Windows 2008

on

Ex   e examples for

W   that these will

su

Tl   ᴇe 3.1. This tab

ca   also be used to

teɪ

Figure 3.1: *Windows Task Manager, Applications View*

The next screen is the *Processes* view (Figure 3.2). The *Processes* view is quite useful; it shows either personal processes or all processes on the server. The good thing about the *Processes* view is that it can be sorted by any of the headings. For example, if CPU is chosen, it will show what processes are using what percent CPU.

This is the same with *Memory*; if sorting by *Memory*, the list will show high to low usage, then low to high if the heading is clicked again. It is also possible to sort by process name or username. Quite handy, right? Processes can also be killed from this screen by highlighting the process and clicking *End Process,* but be careful!

usage (RAM), CPU usage, processes, users, and network. The process list can be sorted by any of the headings, revealing which ones are using the most CPU, memory, and so on. They can also be sorted alphabetically. Several of the tabs are customizable, allowing many headings to be added to the display.

The quickest way to get to the Task Manager is to right click the task bar and select *Task Manager*. The other way is to type *Control-Alt-Delete* and select *Task Manager*. There are several items that the Task Manager can display: Applications (programs the session is running), Processes (personally or the entire server), Services (this tab is on Windows 2008 only), Performance, Networking, and Users.

Examples of each screen type are shown next. These are examples for Windows 2008, but Windows 2003 is similar enough that these will suffice for both, and the differences will be noted.

The first example is the *Applications* view, as seen in Figure 3.1. This tab can be used to see what applications are running, and can also be used to terminate applications.

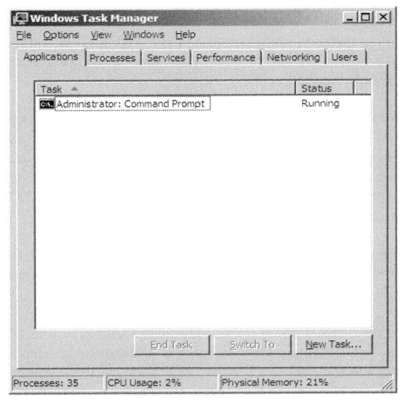

Figure 3.1: *Windows Task Manager, Applications View*

The next screen is the *Processes* view (Figure 3.2). The *Processes* view is quite useful; it shows either personal processes or all processes on the server. The good thing about the *Processes* view is that it can be sorted by any of the headings. For example, if CPU is chosen, it will show what processes are using what percent CPU.

This is the same with *Memory*; if sorting by *Memory*, the list will show high to low usage, then low to high if the heading is clicked again. It is also possible to sort by process name or username. Quite handy, right? Processes can also be killed from this screen by highlighting the process and clicking *End Process,* but be careful!

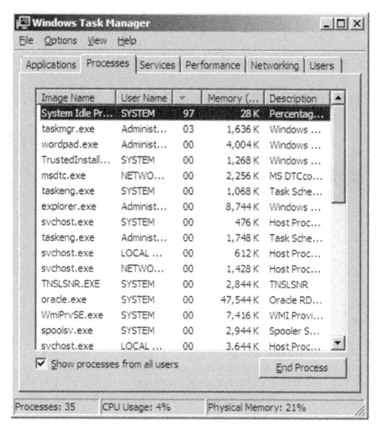

Figure 3.2: *Windows Task Manager, Processes View*

This display is also customizable. Columns can be added or removed from the display. Just go to *View* and choose *Select Columns*, shown in Figure 3.3.

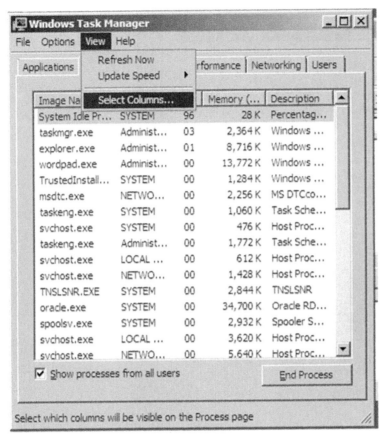

Figure 3.3: *Windows Task Manager, View Screen*

A selection screen of items available to display appears. Simply choose which ones are desired and select *OK* at the bottom.

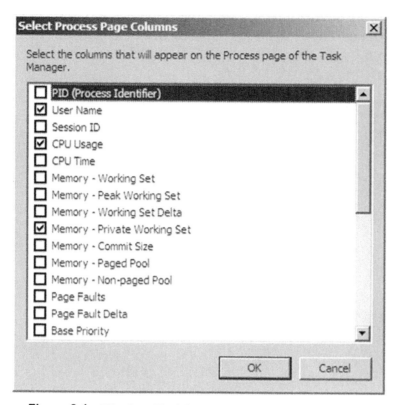

Figure 3.4: *Windows Task Manager, Selection Screen*

The next tab is the *Services* tab. The *Services* tab (Windows 2008 only) displays all of the Windows services on the server and their status (running, stopped), as can be seen in Figure 3.5. Clicking on the *Services* button will go to the *Services* screen, where the Windows services can be controlled (stop/start/etc.). Windows services will be covered in more detail in Chapter 6.

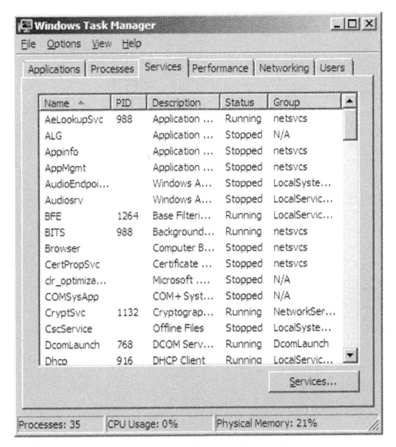

Figure 3.5: *Windows Task Manager, Services Screen*

Next is the *Performance* tab. The *Performance* tab shows CPU utilization and memory usage. This is a very useful screen to check server performance at a glance. Our only wish was that it would include disk I/O. However, if the Resource Monitor (Windows 2008 only) is clicked, it will go to the Windows Performance Monitor, which can indeed show disk I/O.

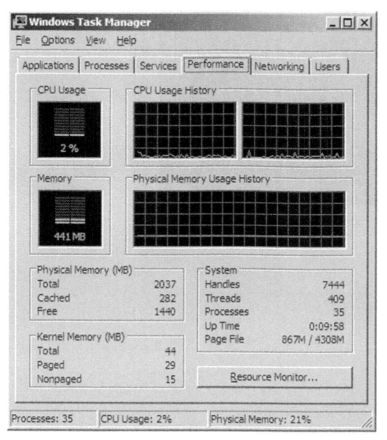

Figure 3.6: *Windows Task Manager, Performance Screen*

The next tab is *Networking*. The *Networking* tab displays utilization information for all NICs on the server, as shown in the next figure (Figure 3.7). This is a good way to check network traffic coming through the server.

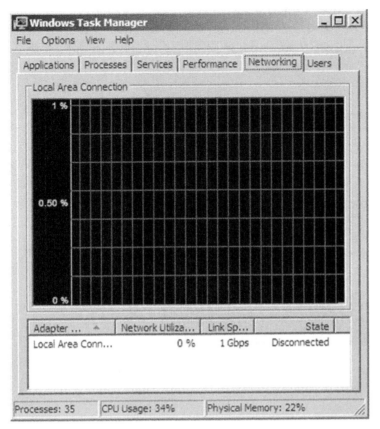

Figure 3.7: *Windows Task Manager, Networking Screen*

The final tab is the *Users* tab. The *Users* tab displays all the connected users on the server. The display is able to be sorted by the columns, and users can be disconnected and logged off using the screen shown in Figure 3.8.

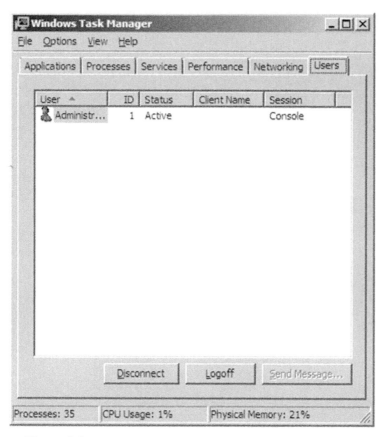

Figure 3.8: *Windows Task Manager, Users Screen*

Again, about the only thing the Task Manager really does not show is disk activity. For disk I/O we use the Windows Performance Monitor, which will be discussed in the following section.

Windows Performance Monitor

In order to run the Performance Monitor in Windows 2003, go to *Start*, *Administrative Tools*, and *Performance* as seen in Figure 3.9 below. In Windows 2008, it is found the same way but is called Resource and Performance Monitor.

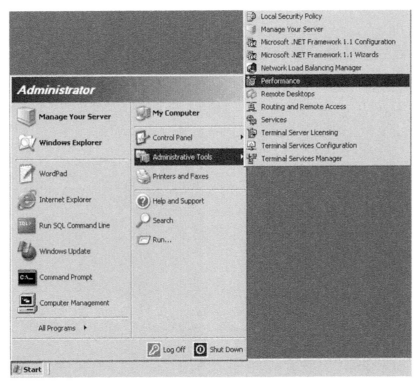

Figure 3.9: *Navigating to Windows Performance Monitor, Windows 2003*

Alternatively, in Windows 2008, it can also be accessed by clicking on the *Resource Monitor* button in Task Manager, under the *Performance* tab as seen in Figure 3.10 below.

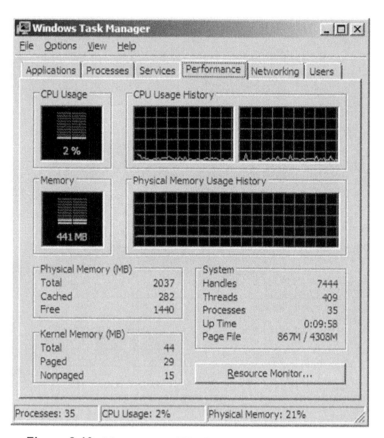

Figure 3.10: *Navigating to Windows Performance Monitor, Windows 2008*

When the program opens in Windows 2003, three basic measures are displayed: Pages/Sec, Percent Processor, and Average Disk Queue Length, as seen in Figure 3.11 below.

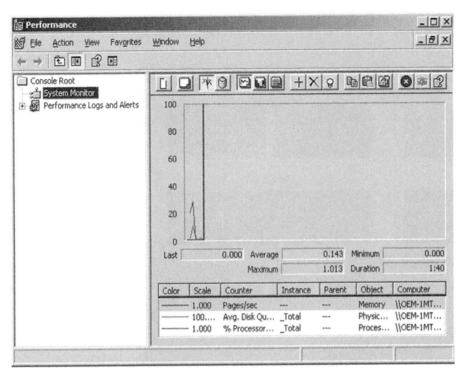

Figure 3.11: *System Monitor, + Button, Categories View Screen*

In Windows 2008, the display is a bit different. The main screen will display a very nice summary of CPU, Disk, Network, and Memory statistics, as shown in Figure 3.12.

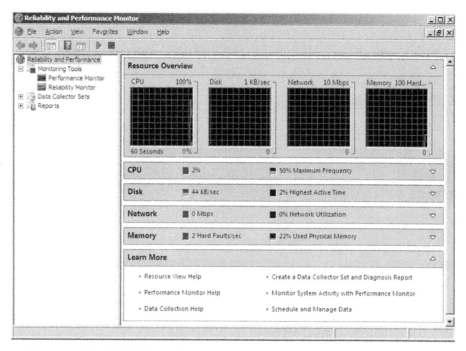

Figure 3.12: *CPU, Disk, Network, and Memory Statistics*

In the Windows 2008 *Performance Monitor/Resource Monitor*, each area on the screen can be expanded upon to give a quick summary of each category – CPU, Disk, Network, and Memory, as seen in the next sequence of screen shots.

Note that for CPU, each running image has a line of information, and each heading can be sorted upon by clicking on the heading.

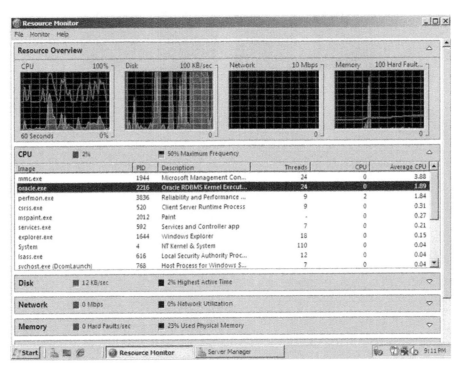

Figure 3.13: *Resource Monitor, Resource Overview*

For Disk, each image has a line of information, and again it is sortable by each heading. Note that you can see read and write rates as well as response time in milliseconds.

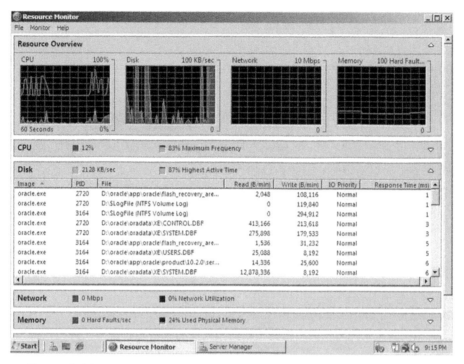

Figure 3.14: *Resource Monitor, Resource Overview*

The *Memory* screen works the same way, as does the *Network* screen. Note the hard fault column, which would indicate memory being exhausted and the server needing to page to disk.

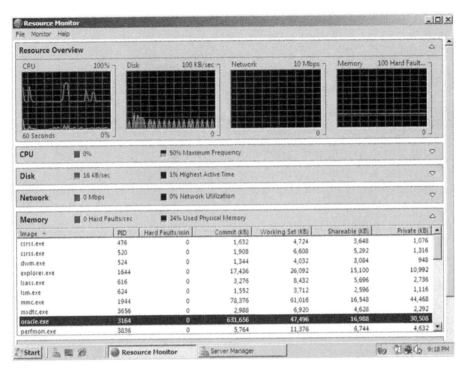

Figure 3.15: *Resource Monitor, Resource Overview*

Windows for Oracle DBAs

Adding Counters in the Performance Monitor

In order to advance to the Performance Monitor screen, which is the default in Windows 2003, click on *Performance Monitor* in the left hand pane. The display, as shown in Figure 3.16, will appear.

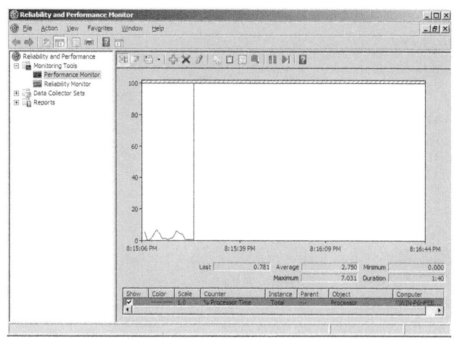

Figure 3.16: *Performance Monitor, + Button*

There are several other measurements available; for both Windows 2003 and 2008, clicking on the + button lists all the major categories, called Performance Objects, such as Processor, Physical Disk, Logical Disk, and such.

In Windows 2003, the *Add Counters* screen looks as follows (Figure 3.17).

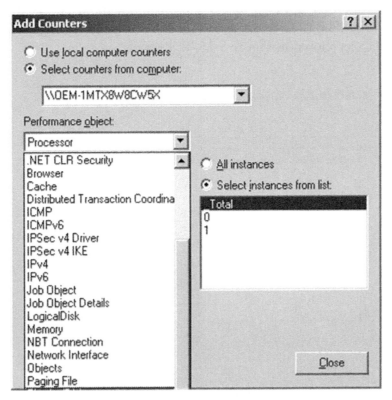

Figure 3.17: *Performance Object, Select Counter*

Once a Performance Object has been selected, the counter that should be used is selected, as seen in Figure 3.18.

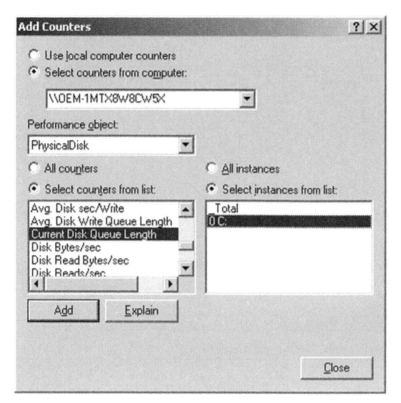

Figure 3.18: *Performance Object, Add Counter*

Once the counter is selected, click the *Add* button, and the counter will be added to the chart (Figure 3.19).

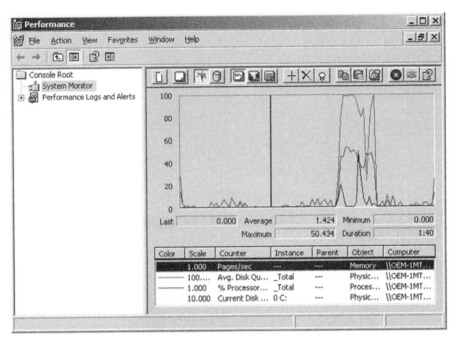

Figure 3.19: *System Monitor, Performance Measures*

Generally, the most useful counters for an Oracle system are:

- Physical Disk/Current Disk Queue Length, Physical Disk/% Disk Time – both per device

- % Processor

- % CPU

An example of these measures is shown in Figure 3.19.

In Windows 2008, the screens appear a bit differently, but counters are added a similar way. The + button is still used to add counters (Figure 3.20), but in Windows 2008, a different *Add Counters* screen appears (Figure 3.21).

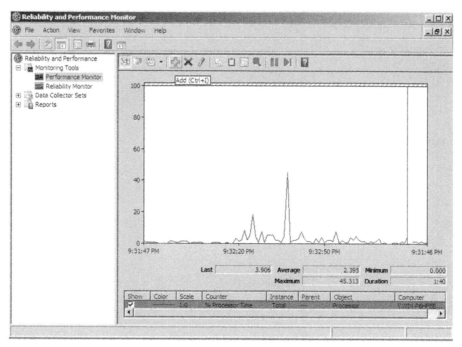

Figure 3.20: *Windows 2008 Performance Monitor*

The main categories are listed in the left pane, as seen in Figure 3.21.

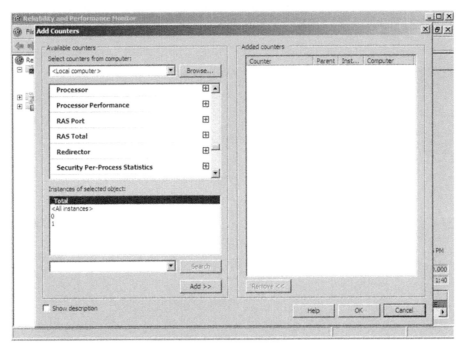

Figure 3.21: *Windows 2008 Performance Monitor, Add Counters*

In this example, we are choosing *Physical Disk* and the subcategory *% Disk Time,* as shown in Figure 3.22.

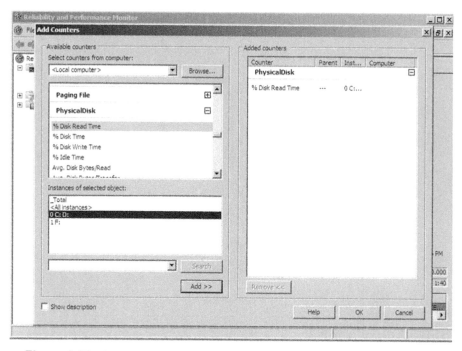

Figure 3.22: *Windows 2008 Performance Monitor, Add Counters*

Once *OK* is clicked, the chosen counters are displayed, as shown in Figure 3.23.

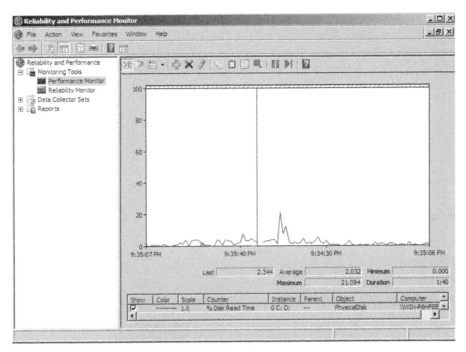

Figure 3.23: *Windows 2008 Performance Monitor, Add Counters*

Now that we have covered adding counters using the Performance Monitor, we will move on to examine how to save settings to a file in the Performance Monitor.

Saving Settings to a File

The Performance Monitor allows saving selected settings to a file for use next time it is run. It works the same way in Windows 2003 and 2008. The following examples are using 2003 screenshots, but the procedure is the same using 2008.

In order to do this, select all the settings that should be displayed, as explained previously. Then go to *File, Save As* (as shown in Figure 3.24), and choose a name and folder. The default folder is *Windows\system32*, but it would make sense to save these to a separate folder so it is easier to find them later. In this example, the folder is *C:\performance*.

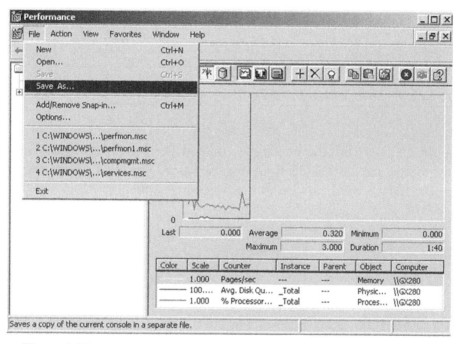

Figure 3.24: *Performance Monitor, Saving Settings to a File*

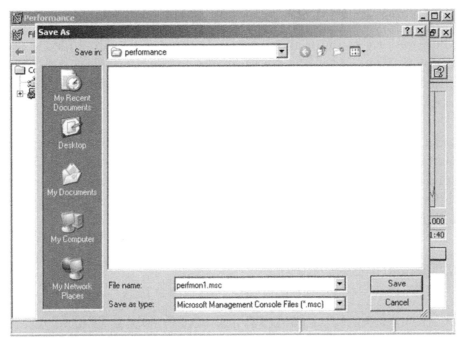

Figure 3.25: *Performance Monitor, Saving Setting to a File*

Once the file is saved, the next time you run Performance Monitor, the same settings can be loaded by going to *Start, Open*, and navigating to where the file is stored, as seen in the following sequence.

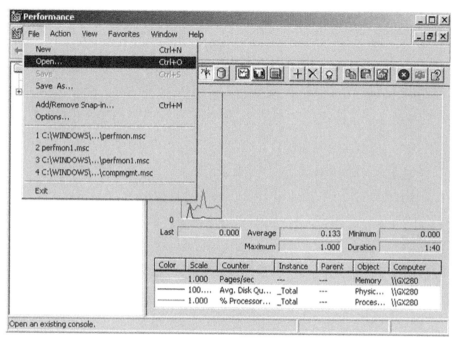

Figure 3.26: *Performance Monitor, Load Same Settings*

Figure 3.27: *Performance Monitor, Load Same Settings*

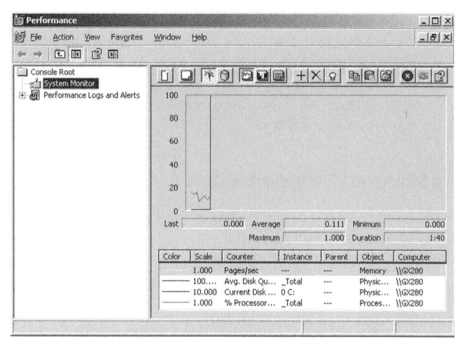

Figure 3.28: *Performance Monitor, Load Same Settings*

Now that we see how to save and load settings from a file, let's take a look at how to save sessions to a logfile in both Windows 2003 and 2008.

Saving Sessions to a Logfile

Performance Monitor also allows saving the counters to a logfile, which can be played back later. When doing this, it can also be run in the background so there is no need to stay logged on for the counter to continue running. Monitoring overall server performance is a critical part of efficiently running an Oracle database, since bottlenecks in CPU, Memory, and Disk I/O directly affect database performance.

Note! Many of these server metrics are saved inside Oracle if you have installed the Oracle STATSPACK utility, or if you have purchased access to the Automatic Workload Repository (AWR)

Saving logfiles is done differently in Windows 2003 versus Windows 2008. Instructions for each follow.

Saving Settings to a File in Windows 2003

To save setting in Windows 2003, begin by clicking on *Counter Logs* in the left hand pane, as seen in Figure 3.29.

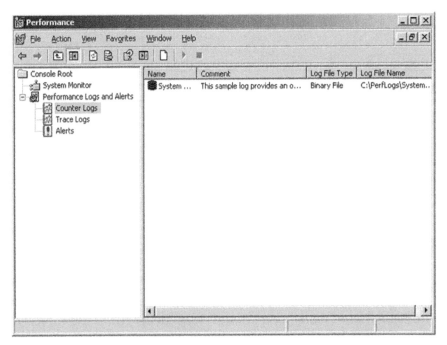

Figure 3.29: *Windows 2003 Performance Monitor, Counter Logs*

Next, right click the blank space in the right pane and select *New Log Settings*, as shown in Figure 3.30.

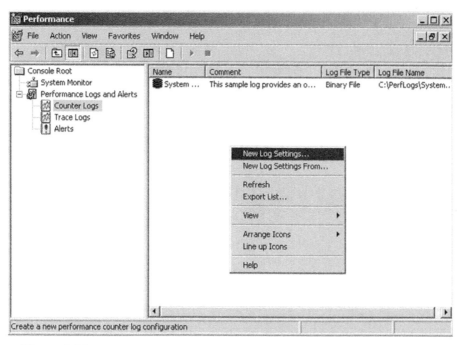

Figure 3.30: *Windows 2003 Performance Monitor, New Log Settings*

It will then ask for a name, as shown in Figure 3.31. This is the title of the monitor session so it can be referred to later.

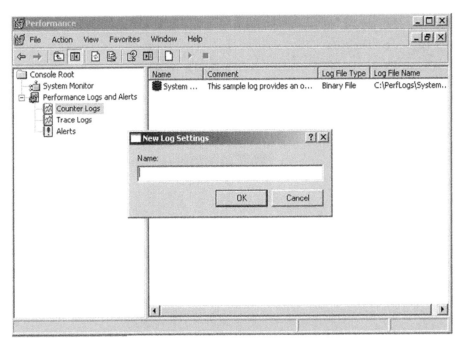

Figure 3.31: *Windows 2003 Performance Monitor, New Log Settings, Filename*

Type in the name to be used as a filename, fully qualified if so desired.

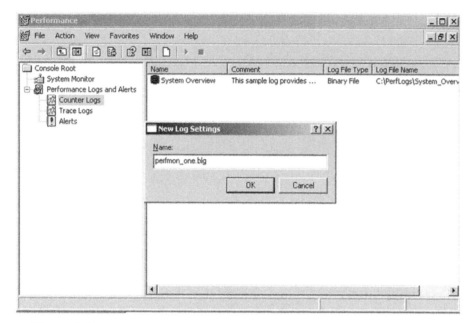

Figure 3.32: *Windows 2003 Performance Monitor, New Log Settings, Filename*

Once the name has been entered and *OK* is clicked, the next screen (Figure 3.33) will appear. This is where you choose the counters to use, which works the same as described in the beginning of this section.

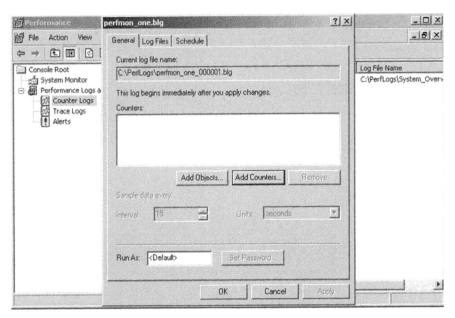

Figure 3.33: *Windows 2003 Performance Monitor, Add Counters*

In this example, we will choose current disk queue length as a counter (Figure 3.34).

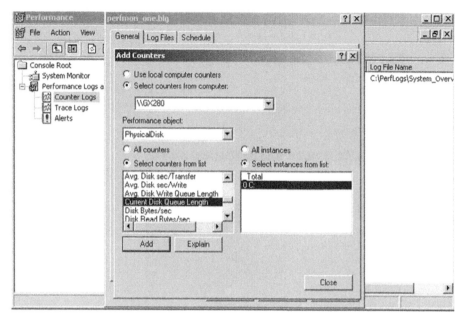

Figure 3.34: *Windows 2003 Performance Monitor, Add Counters*

Once the measure has been chosen, the counter will be displayed. There will be an option to select interval and unit; in this example, the interval is 15 seconds, as seen in Figure 3.35. Therefore, a measure of current disk queue length for the C: drive will be recorded every 15 seconds.

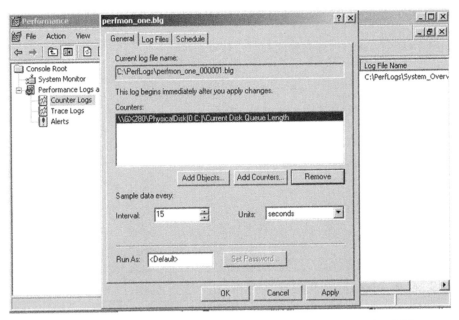

Figure 3.35: *Windows 2003 Performance Monitor, Select Interval and Unit*

Once the counters and intervals have been selected, the *Schedule* tab can be used to select when to start and end recording. In this example, we started at 6:00 AM and ended at 5:00 PM, as shown in Figure 3.36.

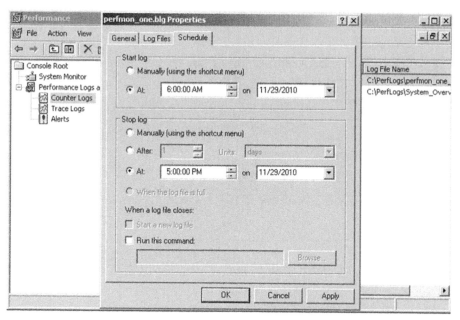

Figure 3.36: *Windows 2003 Performance Monitor, Select Interval and Unit*

Lastly, the *Log Files* tab can be used to define the file type to output, as shown in Figure 3.37. The default is a binary log file, which can be read by Performance Monitor to play back. Other choices include delimited text files for use in spreadsheets or input to databases, as well as direct input to a SQL Server database.

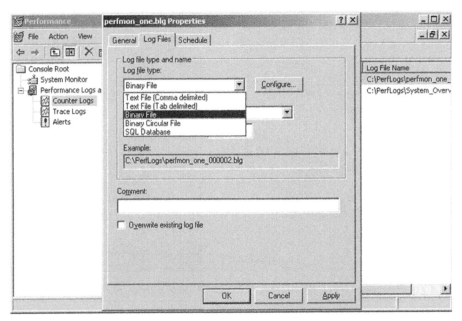

Figure 3.37: *Windows 2003 Performance Monitor, Log Files*

Clicking *OK* will exit the selections and schedule the monitor to start collecting data at the chosen time. There is no need to stay logged in; the Performance Monitor will run as scheduled even if you are logged out.

Saving Monitor Sessions to a File in Windows 2008

In order to do this in Windows 2008, it works a bit differently. Here, it's necessary to select all the settings you want to record first, whereas in

2003 these are selected later. These choices are the set of statistics that will be recorded into the file.

To begin, right click *Performance Monitor* in the left pane and select *Create New Data Collector Set.* Choose a name and enter it (Figure 3.38).

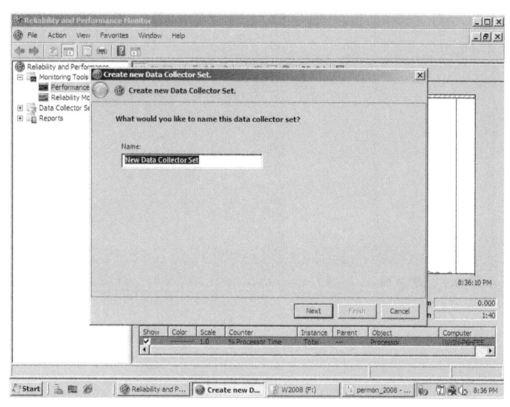

Figure 3.38: *Windows 2008 Performance Monitor, New Data Collector Set*

The data collector set has now been created and is displayed, as seen in Figure 3.39 below, with a status of stopped.

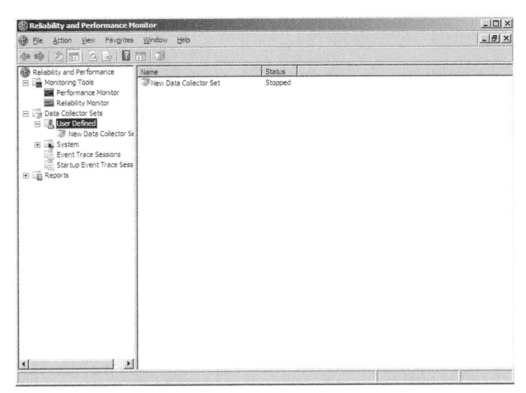

Figure 3.39: *Windows 2008 Performance Monitor, New Data Collector Set*

This can be scheduled or run by right clicking the name and selecting the *Schedule* tab.

Now that we have covered saving monitor sessions in Windows 2003 and 2008, let's move on to discuss playing back monitor sessions.

Playing Back Monitor Sessions

Now that we know how to save sessions to a file, we need a way to play them back. Thankfully, this works the same way in both 2003 and 2008. In either case, clicking the *View Log Data* icon in the main Performance Monitor screen will bring up the required popup box.

In Windows 2003, it looks like Figure 3.40 below.

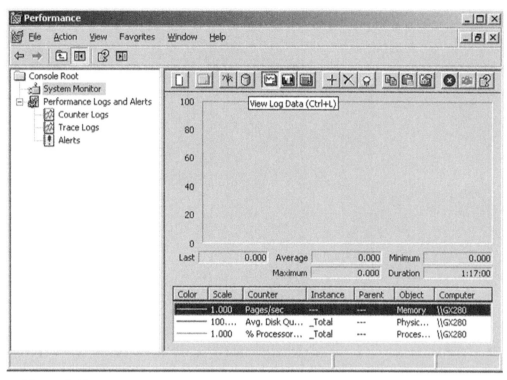

Figure 3.40: *Windows 2003 Performance Monitor, View Log Data*

In Windows 2008, it looks like Figure 3.41.

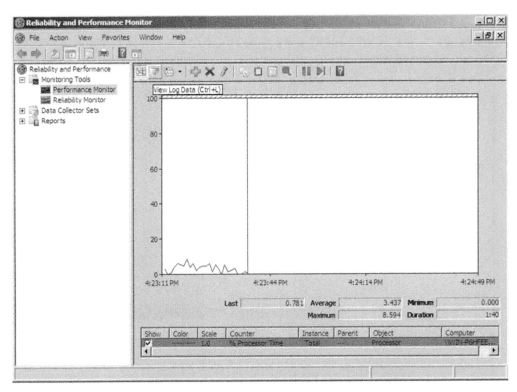

Figure 3.41: *Windows 2008 Performance Monitor, View Log Data*

Once we get past the icon, the rest of the screens are identical. Therefore, Windows 2008 screens will be used for the rest of the example.

The next screen will be the *Performance Monitor Properties* screen (Figure 3.42). Here we will choose the *Source* tab and click the *Log files:* button.

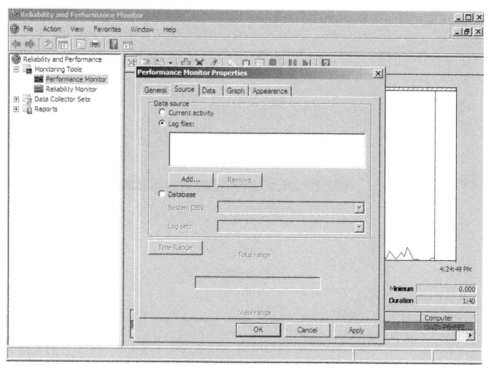

Figure 3.42: *Performance Monitor, Properties Screen*

Next, click *Add* and the *Select Log File* screen popup appears (Figure 3.43). Navigate to the folder where the logfile was saved to, and click *Open*.

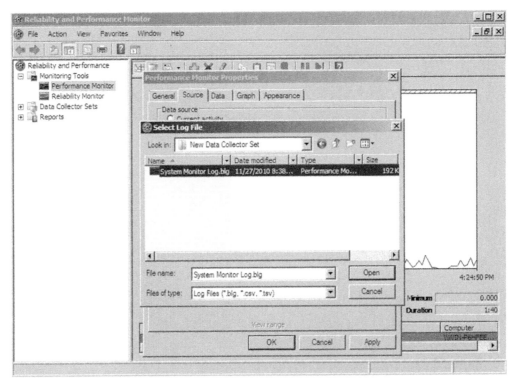

Figure 3.43: *Performance Monitor, Select Log File*

The popup will disappear and the previous screen will now have the logfile displayed in the pane, as seen in Figure 3.44.

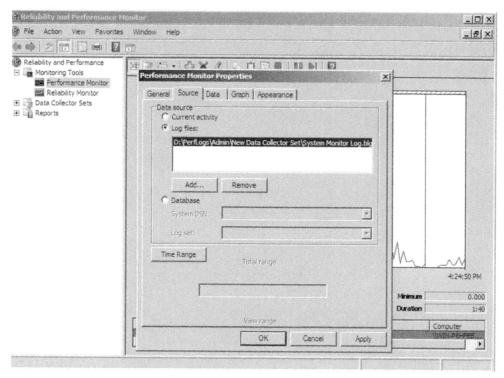

Figure 3.44: *Performance Monitor, Log File*

Click *OK*, and the playback screen will appear as seen in Figure 3.45.

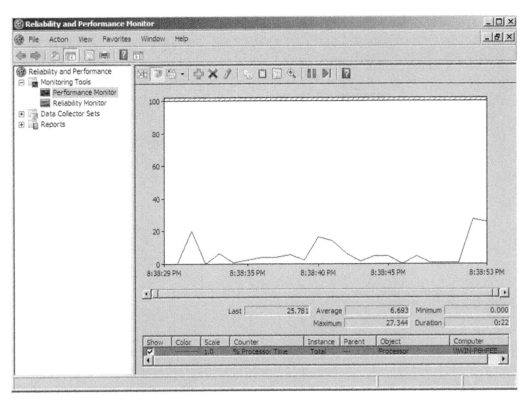

Figure 3.45: *Performance Monitor, Playback Screen*

Keeping a Performance Monitor session running can assist in pinpointing bottlenecks on your system.

Windows Event Viewer

Windows logs events to various logs called Event Logs. These are split into different types. In Windows 2003 and 2008, they are the System, Application, and Security logs. These are defined by Microsoft as follows:

- **Application log**: The Application log contains events logged by applications or programs. For example, a database program might record a file error in the Application log. The program developer decides which events to record.

- **System log**: The System log contains events logged by the Windows operating system components. For example, the failure of a driver or other system component to load during startup is recorded in the System log. The event types logged by system components are predetermined by the Windows operating system.

- **Security log**: The Security log can record security events such as valid and invalid logon attempts as well as events related to resource use, such as creating, opening, or deleting files. An administrator can specify what events are recorded in the Security log. For example, if you have enabled logon auditing, attempts to log on to the system are recorded in the Security log.

In a nutshell, any Server type events are in the System log, Security events such as Windows logins/logouts are in the Security log, and Application related events (including Oracle) are in the Application log. Relatively simple to remember!

In Windows 2008, there are also *Setup* and *Forwarded* Events. These are outside our scope and need not be reviewed here.

For Oracle, some additional information is important to know. Oracle Database events are recorded in the Windows Application event log, accessible via the Event Viewer.

Event number 34 signifies an Oracle audit trail event. These are recorded if the parameter AUDIT_TRAIL is set to *db* (true) or *os* in the *init.ora* file or *spfile*. *OS* enables database auditing and causes audited records to be written to Event Viewer. *DB* enables auditing and causes audit records to be written to the database audit trail table (SYS.AUD$), but unlike UNIX, some records are still written to Windows Application event log. Event numbers other than 34 specify general database activities, such as an instance being started or stopped.

The *init* parameter AUDIT_FILE_DEST is not supported in Windows and should not be added to the initialization parameter file, as it is not supported in the Windows versions of Oracle.

In Windows 2003 and 2008, the Event Viewer works much the same way. The screens differ a bit, but the functionality is similar.

In both flavors of Windows, the Event Viewer is accessed from the *Computer Management* screen. The easiest way to access that is to go to *Start*, right click *My Computer*, and select *Manage*. This looks as follows (Figure 3.46):

Figure 3.46: *Accessing the Event Viewer*

Windows 2003 Event Viewer

In Windows 2003, the Event Viewer is under System Tools, as seen in Figure 3.47. The Application, Security, and System log choices are displayed by either clicking on Event Viewer, in which case they appear in the right pane, or by expanding the Event Viewer (clicking on the + next to it), in which case they appear below. In the example, both are shown.

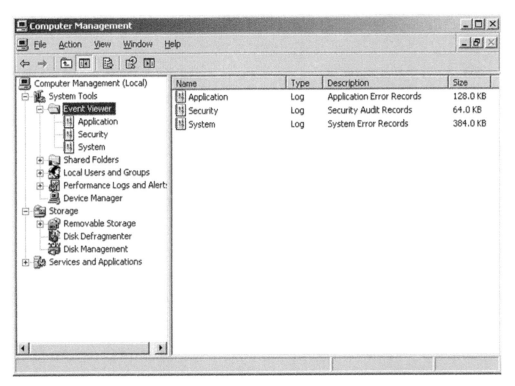

Figure 3.47: *Windows 2003 System Tools, Event Viewer*

Once a log type is clicked, in this case Application, the listing of all that type of event is displayed (Figure 3.48). The list can be sorted by any column by clicking the heading. Also, the result set can be filtered by clicking *View* and selecting *Filter* at the top of the screen.

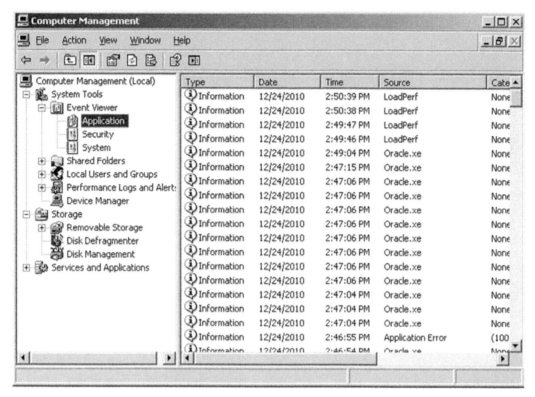

Figure 3.48: *Windows 2003 Event Viewer, Display Events*

In order to see more detail on an entry, simply select the one you want and click on it. The detail screen will appear (Figure 3.49). Clicking on the up and down arrows on the right of the detail screen will navigate you through the next or previous entries.

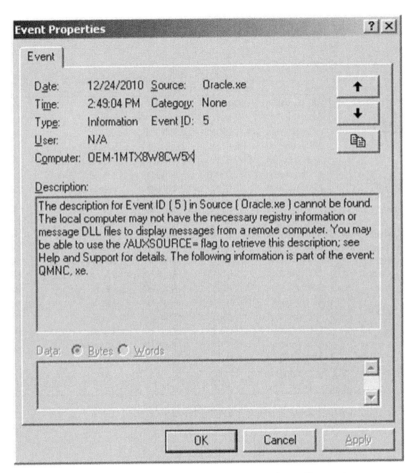

Figure 3.49: *Windows 2003 Event Viewer, Event Properties*

Windows 2008 Event Viewer

In Windows 2008, the Event Viewer is under Diagnostics, and then Windows Logs, as seen in Figure 3.50. The Event Log choices are displayed by either clicking on *Windows Logs*, in which case they appear in the right pane, or by expanding the Event Viewer (clicking on the + next to it), in which case they appear below. In the example, Windows Logs is expanded, and System Log was chosen.

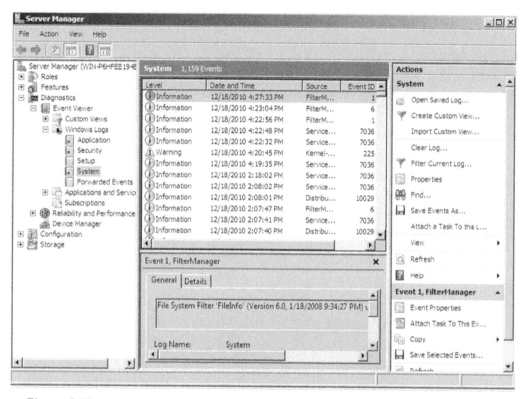

Figure 3.50: *Windows 2008 Event Viewer*

As in Windows 2003, once the log is selected, the list of entries appears in the right pane (more like center in this case!). Here in Windows 2008, mousing over an entry brings up a summary of the detail in the bottom pane, as seen in Figure 3.51.

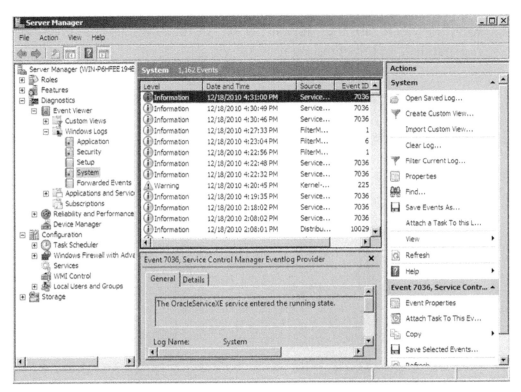

Figure 3.51: *Windows 2008 Event Viewer, Summary Detail*

Clicking on the entry brings up the full detail in a separate popup window (Figure 3.52). Again, as in Windows 2003, the arrows on the right will navigate you up and down the list.

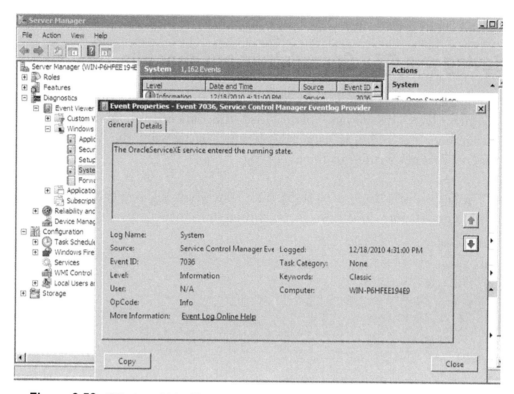

Figure 3.52: *Windows 2008 Event Viewer, Event Properties*

Clicking the *Copy* button at the bottom left will copy the details to the Windows clipboard, so it can be pasted into a document or file. The paste output for the above screen is below.

```
Log Name:        System
Source:          Service Control Manager
Date:            12/18/2010 4:30:49 PM
Event ID:        7036
Task Category:   None
Level:           Information
Keywords:        Classic
User:            N/A
Computer:        WIN-P6HFEE194E9
```

```
Description:
The OracleServiceXE service entered the running state.
Event Xml:
<Event xmlns="http://schemas.microsoft.com/win/2004/08/events/event">
  <System>
    <Provider Name="Service Control Manager" Guid="{555908D1-A6D7-4695-8E1E-
26931D2012F4}" EventSourceName="Service Control Manager" />
```

Saving to a CSV Spreadsheet or Other File Type

Another handy thing is the ability to save the event log out to a .csv or
other file. This allows you to load the data into a table, view it all
together, etc. This is especially handy for viewing the Oracle-related
items that get written to the event log.

The way this is done is to right click whichever log you care to save off,
and choose *Save All Events As*, as shown in Figure 3.53.

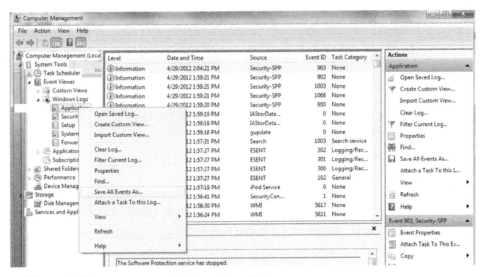

Figure 3.53: *Saving to a CSV or Other Filetype*

You then can select what file type you want from the dropdown, the filename, and where you want it saved, as seen in Figure 3.54.

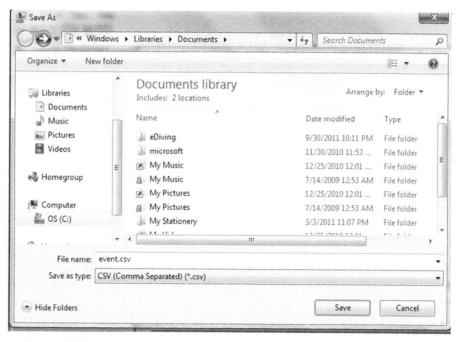

Figure 3.54: *Saving to a CSV or Other File type*

Summary

Two very important tools, the Performance Monitor and Task Manager, were examined in this chapter.

The Windows Task Manager is used to find out everything that is happening on the server including what processes and applications are running, CPU utilization and memory usage among other items.
Windows Performance Monitor is primarily used to monitor disk activity.

Now we will move on to cover the Windows Registry, including how to export an entire registry or an individual key.

The Windows Registry CHAPTER

4

Introduction

There is something about the inherent complexity of the Windows Registry that strikes fear into the hearts of many – so much so that they tend to avoid it completely. There is good reason, for if the registry is tinkered with and the DBA is not careful, the result may be an unbootable Windows system!

Take heart, though! If care is taken with some steps to allow recovery, the danger of editing the registry is not insurmountable. Knowing your way around the registry is actually a very handy skill.

The following topics will be covered in this chapter:

- Running the Registry Editor
- Exporting the registry
- Exporting individual keys
- Restoring an individual key from an export
- Oracle-related registry entries

We will begin with a brief overview of the Windows Registry.

Functionality of the Windows Registry

In a nutshell, the Windows Registry is a primitive database repository. The repository contains all of the Windows parameters, plus external "system" parameters for all programs running on the server, including some parameters for the Oracle database.

The concept of the Windows Registry can be compared roughly to the Oracle *spfile* or *pfile*. While the *spfile* or *pfile* is the repository for all of the internal Oracle Database parameters, the Windows Registry is the repository for all the system parameters and settings for the server.

The Windows Registry replaces all of the *.ini* files that earlier versions of Windows used for saving configuration information for the system and its applications.

The actual files that make up the registry are in *C:\Windows\System32\config* for all the registry areas except HKEY_LOCAL_USER. The HKEY_LOCAL_USER files are in *C:\Windows\Profiles\<username>*.

Large books have been written on using the Windows Registry, but the purpose of this book is to show what we need to know as it relates to Oracle, so we will only delve into what is relevant to run Oracle on Windows.

Generally, any time an application is installed, such as Oracle, an entry is created in the registry containing the pertinent values needed for it to run. These are placed in sections called "hives", generally under the root key:

HKEY_LOCAL_MACHINE\Software

The main root keys in the Registry are:
- *HKEY_CLASSES_ROOT*
- *HKEY_CURRENT_USER*
- *HKEY_LOCAL_MACHINE*
- *HKEY_USERS*

- *HKEY_CURRENT_CONFIG*

The only key we will focus on is *HKEY_LOCAL_MACHINE*, since this is where everything we need to run Oracle is located.

1. *HKEY_LOCAL_MACHINE* has several subclasses. The ones of interest to us are Software and System.

2. *HKEY_LOCAL_MACHINE\Software\Oracle* is where all the Oracle keys are kept.

3. *HKEY_LOCAL_MACHINE\System\CurrentControlSet\Services* is where all of the Windows services (including Oracle) are defined.

Now that we know the function and structure of the registry, let's see how to change registry entries.

Running the Registry Editor

The quickest way to get to the Registry Editor is to click *Start* then *Run*, and enter *regedit.exe* as the program name. Alternately, open Windows Explorer and navigate to *C:\Windows* and click on *regedit.exe*. In Windows 2008, it may be navigated to using Windows Explorer, right clicking, and then choosing *Run as administrator*.

In either Windows 2003 or Windows 2008, the Registry Editor looks the same. Notice the five main keys shown in Figure 4.1.

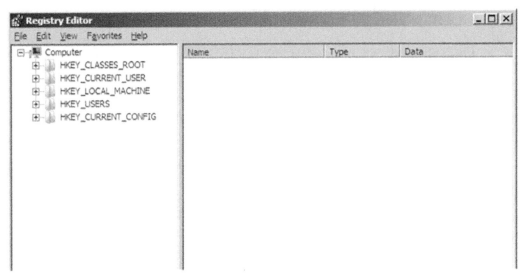

Figure 4.1: *Five Main Keys of Registry Editor*

All DBA's know that you have to take a backup of something before you change it, and the registry is no exception. Let's see how to export a backup copy of the registry.

Taking a Backup of the Registry Keys

One thing that is recommended is to create a folder called *C:\Regsave* and always (always always!) export a copy of the registry to that folder whenever Regedit is run, before anything is changed. That ensures that there is something to go back to. To do this, all that is necessary is to click on *Computer* at the top of the left pane (this highlights it so that the entire computer's registry is exported), click on *File*, and then click *Export* as shown in Figure 4.2.

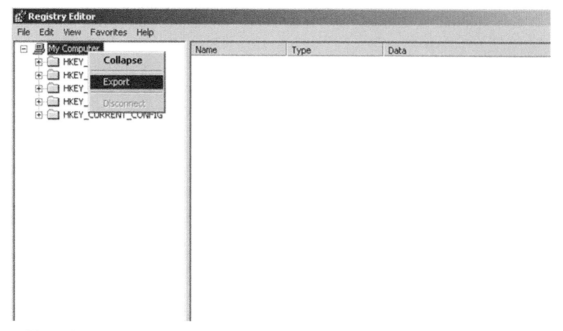

Figure 4.2: *Exporting a Copy of Registry*

Next, navigate to *C:\Regsave*, give it a filename, and then click the *Save* button. We usually use today's date, but use whatever date makes the most sense.

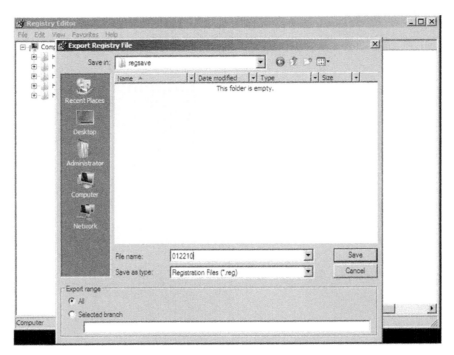

Figure 4.3: *Giving Exported File a Name*

This technique can also be used to save a separate key. For example, if the *HKEY_LOCAL_MACHINE \System \Oracle* key needs to be saved before it is edited, simply highlight that before doing the export. Then either go to *File*, *Export* (as described before) and give it a filename, or right click and choose *Export* and give it a filename. Both options can be seen in the next two screenshots, and both will do the same thing. In Windows, there are always several ways to do the same thing!

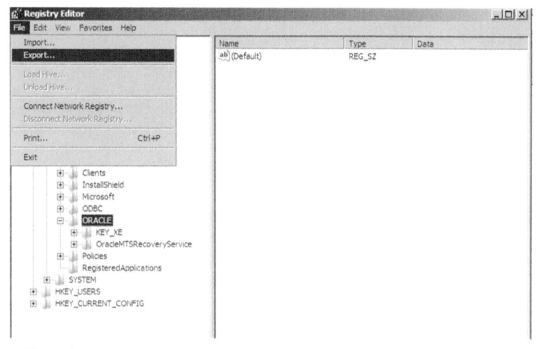

Figure 4.4: *Exporting an Oracle Key: Version 1*

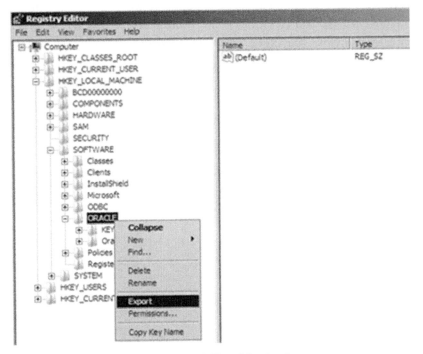

Figure 4.5: *Exporting an Oracle Key: Version 2*

Now that we have an export, we can freely make a change to the registry. In case of a failure, it is easy to restore the registry using the import utility.

Restoring an Individual Key from an Export

OK – a bad thing has happened. Let's assume that we went into the Registry and modified some of the Oracle entries, and now Oracle will not start correctly. However, we were very careful and exported the Oracle key before starting, so there is a quite simple way to put the registry back into the state before we made the change.

First, we need to export the registry again to a different file, just in case. Then start Windows Explorer, navigate to the saved Oracle key export file, and double click on the filename.

Windows knows by the file extension that it is a registry export and imports it back into the registry, overlaying the existing key. It gives a prompt to be sure this should be continued, and then it states that it has successfully restored, as seen in the screens below.

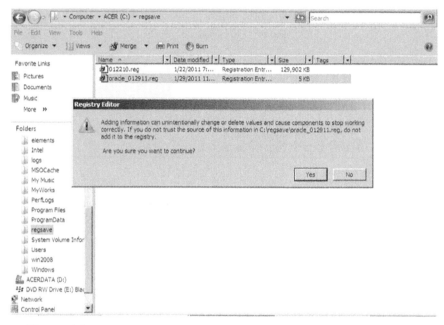

Figure 4.6: *Prompt Before Saving Exported Oracle Key*

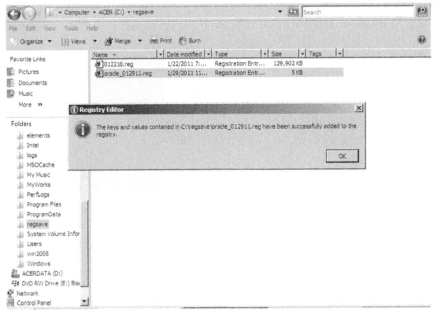

Figure 4.7: *Screen Showing Oracle Key Re-imported*

Now that we know how to back-out changes, let's take a closer look at the Oracle registry keys.

Oracle Related Registry Entries

If navigation to *HKEY_LOCAL_MACHINE*, *Software*, *Oracle* is done, then all the Oracle related registry entries will be seen. The following example shows one Oracle installation and one instance of Oracle called XE. As multiple releases of Oracle and multiple instances are added, this area of the registry will contain all of the information for those as well.

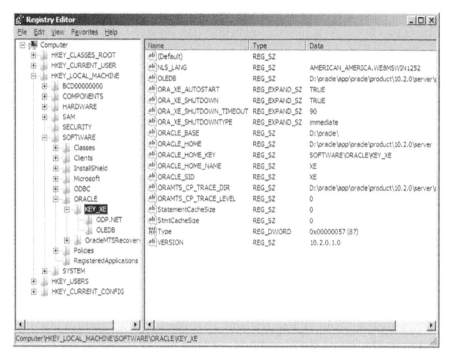

Figure 4.8: *Oracle KEY XE Screen*

Each Oracle instance has a set of registry values associated with it. Usually the key will be called *KEY_sid*, as in the example where it is called *KEY_XE*. The registry values that will most likely be needed to understand and even possibly change are:

- *ora_sid_pfile*: This is the path to the PFILE. If an SPFILE is used, this entry will not exist.

- *ora_sid_autostart*: This tells Windows that the database should be started whenever the Oracle Database service for that instance/SID is started. Generally, this one should be set to TRUE.

- *ora_sid_shutdown*: This one tells Windows to be sure to shut down the database when the Oracle Database service for that instance/SID is stopped. Again, this should almost always be TRUE.

- *ora_sid_shutdown_timeout*: This tells Windows how long to wait for the database to shut down before stopping the service. Default setting is 90 seconds.

- *ora_sid_shutdown_type*: This setting tells Windows what type of shutdown to do (immediate, normal, abort, and such) when the service stops. Generally, this should be set to immediate.

- *ORACLE_HOME*: This is the path to Oracle Home directory

- *NLS_LANG*: This is the NLS Language setting for the server

- *ORACLE_SID*: This contains the name of the Oracle Sid for that key. Again, each Oracle instance will have its own key.

As we see, there are other values as well, but these are the main Oracle parameters.

There is another section in the registry that houses all the keys for the Oracle services that exist on the server. These are located in:

- *HKEY_LOCAL_MACHINE* under the key

- *SYSTEM\CurrentControlSet\Services*, as seen in Figure 4.9.

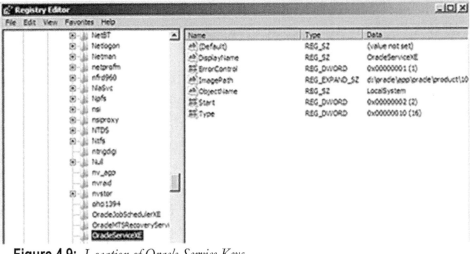

Figure 4.9: *Location of Oracle Service Keys*

For the most part these are left alone, unless for some reason Oracle needs to be manually removed from the server. For that, there are several good Oracle Metalink articles to use for reference!

Summary

Hopefully the Windows Registry has now become comfortable and can be used with a bit more confidence. It is quite useful, especially to see at a glance how Oracle is working on the system.

Now that the Window's Registry has been discussed, let's move on to examine environment variables, including Oracle-related environment variables.

Oracle-related Environment Variables

Introduction

In Windows, as in UNIX and Linux, environment variables exist to predefine items such as directory names, values, and locations that help the batch jobs find the location of important program components. There are many environment variables used in Windows, but for our purposes we will stick to a few of the most commonly needed and used when running Oracle. These are PATH, ORACLE_HOME, and ORACLE_SID. We will also briefly discuss the TNS_ADMIN and SQLPATH environment variables.

Where to find Windows Environment Variables

We will begin by covering where to find Windows environment variables. This process is somewhat different between Windows 2003 and 2008, so these differences will be noted.

One of the easier ways to view the system-level environment variables in all versions of Windows is to go to:

Start → right click *My Computer* → select *Properties*.

This will bring up the *System Properties* screen in Windows 2003, as seen in Figure 5.1.

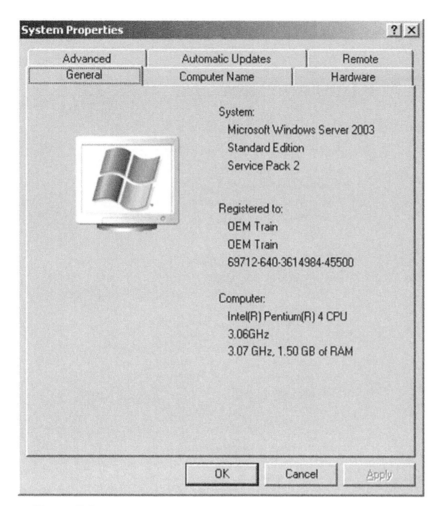

Figure 5.1: *System Properties in Windows 2003*

In Windows 2008, the full screen display will appear, as seen in Figure 5.2.

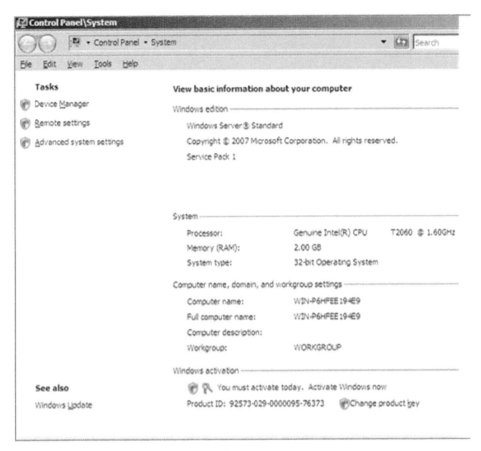

Figure 5.2: *Control Panel\System in Windows 2008*

In both Windows 2003 and 2008, we need to go to the *Advanced* settings. Click on the *Advanced* tab for Windows 2003 or click on *Advanced System Settings* in Windows 2008. In both cases, a screen similar to the one below will appear.

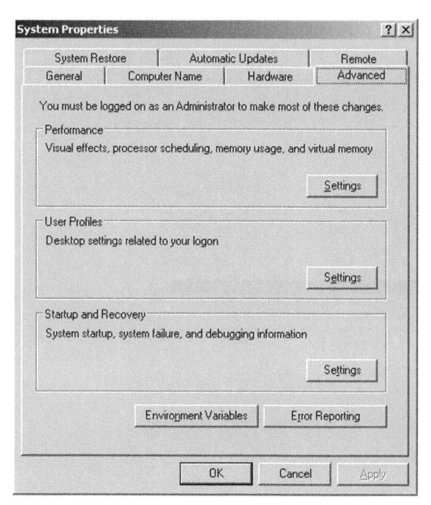

Figure 5.3: *Advanced Settings screen*

Lastly, we click on the *Environment Variables* button on the bottom of the screen. This will display a screen where all the environment variables can be seen and edited. This looks the same on both Windows 2003 and Windows 2008.

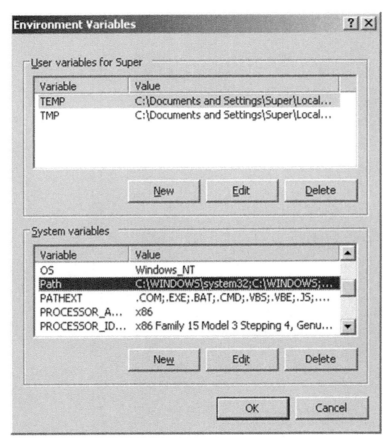

Figure 5.4: *Environment Variables screen*

Generally, the only two variables we need to worry about in this screen are PATH and ORACLE_HOME. ORACLE_SID is stored in the registry.

Another way to see the environment variables is via the command line. Typing *set* at a command prompt will return all the environment variables for that command prompt session.

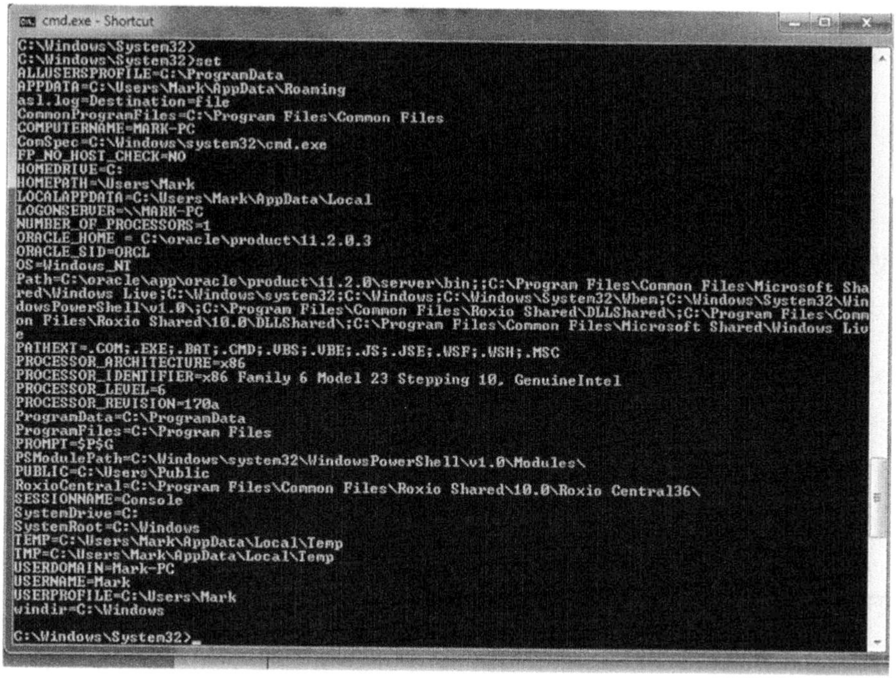

Figure 5.5: *Viewing Environment Variables via the Command Line*

Further, the search can be narrowed by the line:

```
set | findstr "ORACLE"
```

This will execute the *set* command, pipe the output to the *findstr* command, and search for the string ORACLE. This will return any environment variable that has the string ORACLE in it, as seen in Figure 5.6.

Figure 5.6: *Viewing Environment Variables via the Command Line*

Now we will move on to look at each environment variable in detail. The first environment variable we will cover is PATH.

The Windows PATH Variable

The PATH variable is used in Windows in exactly the same way as it is in UNIX and Linux. It is a variable whose contents tells the Operating System where to search for any program or any component that the original program invokes. Because components may exist in multiple locations, the PATH also tells the program in what order to search for the program and its components. The PATH is searched left to right.

> **Beware, the last Oracle Product installed will be the first thing in the PATH.** This can get you in trouble! For example, if the Oracle RDBMS software is installed and later the Oracle Enterprise Manager Agent is installed, Windows will put the Oracle Enterprise Manager Agent directory first in the PATH.

You can change this default PATH sequence by using the *Edit* function on the *Environment Variables* screen, or with the *Environment* tab in Oracle Universal Installer (Figure 5.7).

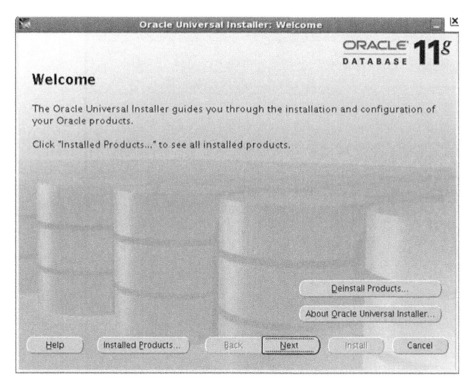

Figure 5.7: *Oracle Universal Installer Welcome screen*

First, click on *Installed Products*. This will bring up the *Inventory* screen, as seen in Figure 5.8. Next, choose the *Environment* tab and use the up/down arrows to select which Oracle Home is first in the PATH, and then click *Apply*.

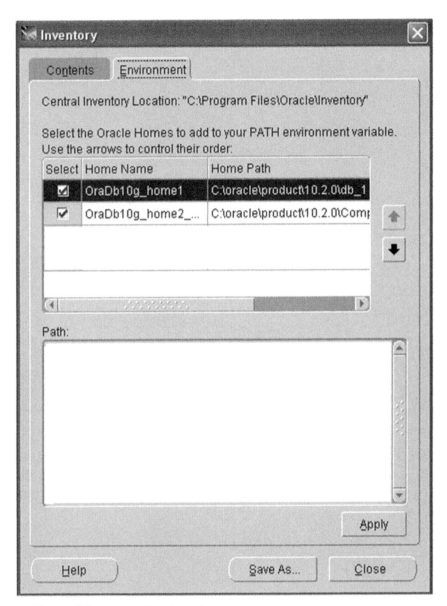

Figure 5.8: *Installed Products, Inventory screen*

The PATH can also be defined at the command line level or in scripts. Simply type:

```
PATH=<whatever folders you require separated by semicolons>
```

Now that PATH has been covered, we will move on to examine the ORACLE_HOME environment variable.

ORACLE_HOME

If multiple releases of Oracle are being run on the same server, it will be necessary to set the ORACLE_HOME local environment variable to use the command line or in your scripts. Setting ORACLE_HOME will ensure that the correct Oracle Software version is accessed when running against the database. This is super critical when multiple versions of Oracle are running on the same Windows Server.

It is also necessary to set ORACLE_HOME at the command prompt when installing patches with the *OPatch* Utility, even if there is only one release of Oracle on the server.

Here is an example from the command prompt:

```
C:>Set ORACLE_HOME=C:\Oracle\product\11.2.0
```

However, in regards to the System Environment Variable that is set in the *Advanced* tab, the situation changes.

The ORACLE_HOME system environment variable will not get reset by an upgrade. More likely, it will be blank, since the Oracle Installer clears it out by default. This can cause TNS Protocol Adapter errors when trying to start the listener, cause ODBC datasources to fail, as well

---

as other problems. Therefore, it is a good practice to check the value following any upgrades or installs.

Oracle recommends that you not set ORACLE_HOME at all, especially if you have multiple Oracle installations on the same machine.

Checking for ORACLE_HOME

It is important to note that the process for checking ORACLE_HOME on a Windows machine is slightly different.

On a Windows Server, the Oracle home information can be found in the system registry. To look at the homes, use this workflow:

Click *Start* → *Run*
   In the Run dialog box, type "regedit" and press *Return*
     The registry will now be displayed
      Expand the folder called
        [HKEY_LOCAL_MACHINE]\SOFTWARE\ORACLE

Now let's examine the ORACLE_SID variable in Windows.

Using ORACLE_SID in Windows

The next environment variable we will discuss is ORACLE_SID. Just like how ORACLE_SID works on UNIX/Linux, the ORACLE_SID identifies the name of a specific database instance and tells the Operating System which Oracle Instance to apply your commands. ORACLE_SID is stored in the registry.

However, any time a database needs to be accessed via the command prompt or with a script, then ORACLE_SID needs to be set. The command line syntax is simply:

```
set ORACLE_SID=sid
```

Note that there are no spaces around the equal sign.
In Windows, the *LOCAL* command can also be used to define the ORACLE_SID.

Now that we have covered the PATH, ORACLE_HOME, and ORACLE_SID environment variables, we will briefly cover setting the SQLPATH environment variable and *tnsnames.ora*.

Setting the SQLPATH Environment Variable

For executing SQL scripts, the default location for SQLPATH is in *$ORACLE_HOME\dbs,* but often SQLPATH is customized to point to a location where multiple instances can access the script collection.

On a Windows PC, the SQLPATH registry entry is located at *HKEY_LOCAL_MACHINE\software\oracle\home0.* This location contains the name of your directory for your SQL script collection.

You can edit your Oracle Windows registry entries with the Windows *regedit* tool.

You can also specify multiple locations in SQLPATH by separating the directories with a semicolon, and the libraries will be searched in the order that they are specified in the SQLPATH registry entry:

```
c:\u01\app\oracle\dbs; c:\u01\app\sql_scripts
```

Finding TNSNAMES.ORA Location

When finding the *tnsnames.ora* location in Windows, look for the TNS_ADMIN registry entry. If TNS_ADMIN is set then you should be able to use a network alias, not the full "(DESCRIPTION..." connect string. The TNS_ADMIN parameter tells Oracle clients where to find the *tnsnames.ora* file.

Also, make sure that TNS_ADMIN is set in your DOS $PATH variable:

```
C:> set TNS_ADMIN=$PATH;ORACLE_HOME\network\admin
```

According to the docs, the precedence in which SQL*Net Configuration files are resolved is:

1. SQL*Net files in present working directory (PWD/CWD)
2. TNS_ADMIN set for each session or by a user-defined DOS script
3. TNS_ADMIN set as a Windows global environment variable
4. TNS_ADMIN as defined in the registry
5. Oracle Net files in %ORACLE_HOME\network\admin
6. (Oracle default location)

Setting the TNS_ADMIN Environment Variable

The TNS_ADMIN environment variable is used to specify the directory location for the *tnsnames.ora* file.
The TNS_ADMIN environment variable can be defined in the following ways:

1. Access the Windows registry by clicking:

Windows for Oracle DBAs

Start → *Run* → *regedit*

2. Add the TNS_ADMIN environment variable to the *HKEY_LOCAL_MACHINE\Software\Oracle\ORACLE_HOME* key by right mouse clicking, and then selecting:

New → *Key* → *String Value*

If you are unsure where to set TNS_ADMIN in the registry, see the *ORACLE_HOME\bin\oracle.key* file which provides the location of the registry key used by executables within that home.

Each time a different Oracle version is installed on Windows, the default location to which SQL*Net files are generated is the *ORACLE_HOME\network\admin* directory.

TNS_ADMIN may also be defined as a system-wide or global variable within the operating system. To do so:

1. Logon as Administrator
2. Click *Start* → *Settings* → *Control Panel*
3. Double click the *SYSTEM* icon
4. From System Properties, select *Environment* tab
5. Highlight *OS* in the list of Systems Variables
6. Change the Variable from OS to TNS_ADMIN
7. Change the Value to the file path where the configuration files will reside. For example: *c:\oranwin\network\admin*.
8. Click *set*, then *apply*
9. Click *OK* to close window

Now let's look at changing the TNS_ADMIN variable.

Changing TNS_ADMIN at the Session Level

For temporary usage, the TNS_ADMIN may also be defined for a given DOS prompt by using the *set* command:

```
C:\> set tns_admin=c:\temp
```

Summary

This chapter has covered several of the most useful environment variables on Windows. PATH, ORACLE_HOME and ORACLE_SID are fundamental to running your Database Server properly.

Many installation and upgrade problems can be avoided by being careful that these are set correctly.

It is also important to understand how to properly set the SQLPATH and TNS_ADMIN environment variables on Windows.

Next, let's move on and cover Windows services.

Windows Services

Introduction to Windows Services

Inside Windows Server, background processes are controlled via "services". These services work much like daemons in UNIX/Linux because they are continuously running programs which sit idle, waiting to be called upon to perform a specific task. From our earlier chapters, we remember that each running service translates to a specific Windows process, and within those processes all the threads are executed.

On Windows, for each Oracle instance there is one Windows service, typically named *OracleServiceSID*, which spawns a process on the service called *oracle.exe*. Inside this process, all the threads are running that support the Oracle instance (i.e. PMON, SMON, etc.), as well as all the user database connections.

This is quite different from UNIX/Linux where the OS controls the dispatching of the background processes. In Windows, Oracle controls the execution priorities of the threads. This gives Oracle more control, because all threads run within a single process, and the service maps to one, and only one service.

These Windows services can be controlled in several ways. These, in the order most used, are:

- The System Management Console
- The command line using *net* commands
- The Windows *sc* command

As such, this chapter will cover the above topics as they relate to Windows services. First we will examine the System Management Console and see how it is used with Oracle Windows.

Services via the System Management Console

Let's begin by covering how Windows services can be accessed via the System Management Console. An easy way to access the Windows services via the System Management Console GUI is to right click *My Computer* and select *Manage*.

This brings up the *System Management* screen. On Windows 2003, expand *Services and Applications* to see the services. Windows 2003 appears as follows:

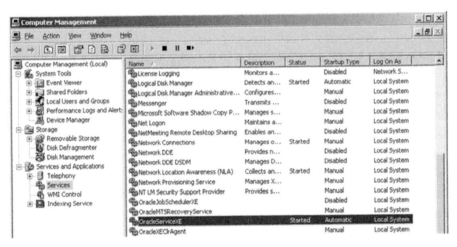

Figure 6.1: *List of Services from System Management Screen, Windows 2003*

Windows 2008 gives a similar display as seen next, except *Configuration* needs to be expanded to show the *Services* screen:

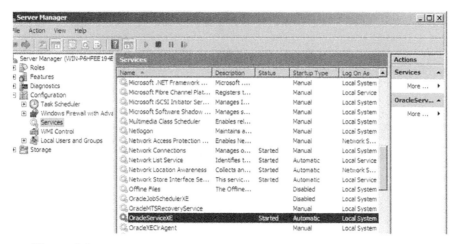

Figure 6.2: *List of Services from System Management Screen, Windows 2008*

In both Windows 2003 and 2008, the rest of the screens are the same. In order to stop, start, restart, or modify the properties on a service, we highlight the service and right click, which gives the appropriate choices. If you prefer, you can do the same function by highlighting the service name and clicking the *Actions* tab at the top of the screen.

The following screen is from Windows 2008, but Windows 2003 works the same way.

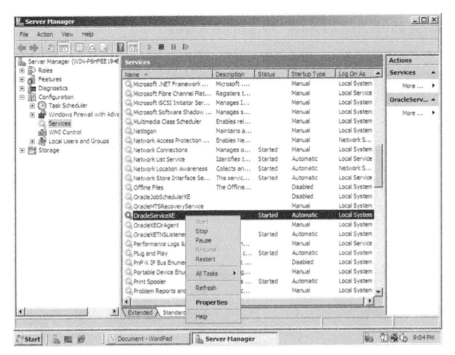

Figure 6.3: *Making Changes on a Service*

Now that we have covered how to get to the services, we will discuss the functionality of the *Properties* screen, beginning with the *General* tab.

The Windows Properties Screen / General Tab

Since the functions of *Stop*, *Start*, and *Restart* are relatively obvious, we will delve into the *Properties* function. In both flavors of Windows, the *Properties* screen looks as follows. The rest of the examples are 2008 since the screen content is essentially the same.

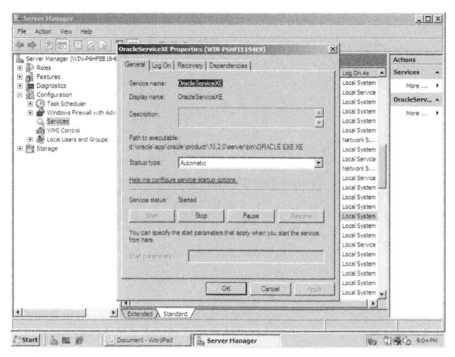

Figure 6.4: *Properties Screen - General Tab*

For the most part, the areas most frequently dealt with are under the *General* tab, specifically *Startup Type*, *Stop*, and *Start*.

Startup Type is a dropdown list on the *General* tab. It allows for setting up the default startup setting, as shown in the next screen.

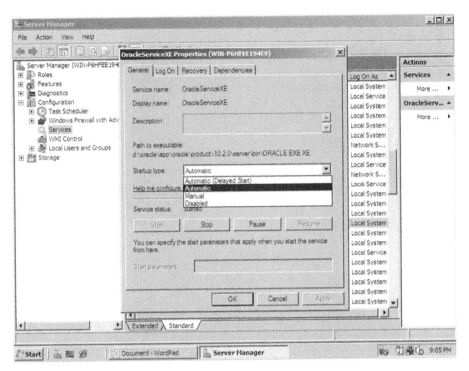

Figure 6.5: *Startup Types*

The *Startup Types* can be set to any of these options:

- *Automatic:* The service starts when the server starts.

- *Manual:* The service is not started when the server starts but can be manually started and stopped.

- *Disabled:* The service is not started when the server starts and cannot be manually started until the service type is changed.

- *Automatic (delayed start):* Windows 2008 only. The service starts when the server starts but the start is delayed until the server is fully booted.

Windows for Oracle DBAs

Automatic Startup of Oracle on Windows

Because Oracle is the world's most flexible and robust database, there are many ways to perform standard system functions such as a Windows automatic startup.

Please note that setting the *startup type=automatic* is only one of several ways that the Oracle DBA will automatically restart an Oracle database after a Windows reboot. The full list of methods for autostarting Oracle includes:

- **Service Properties**: Set the Oracle service to *startup type=automatic*
- **OEM**: Use the Oracle Administration Assistant for Windows or Oracle Enterprise Manager Grid Control.
- **Registry**: Set the registry. Navigate to the key: *HKEY_LOCAL_MACHINE\SOFTWARE\ORACLE\oracle_home _name* and set the key *ORA_SID_AUTOSTART=true*

The next tab under *Properties* is the *Log On* tab, which will be discussed in the following section.

Properties Screen / Log On Tab

The *Log On* tab of the *Properties* screen tells Windows what account, Local or Active Directory, to start the service under. The screen appears as follows:

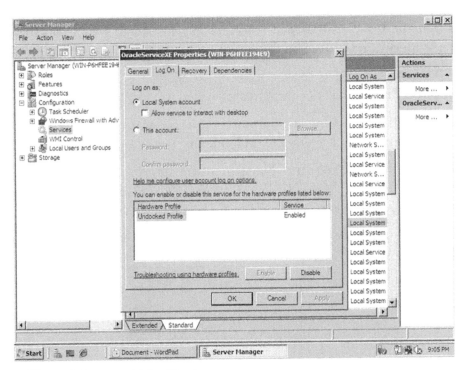

Figure 6.6: *Logon Tab of Services*

The default account Windows uses for services is the Local System Account. If this needs to be changed, click on the *This account:* button, enter the credentials, and click *OK* as seen on the next screen.

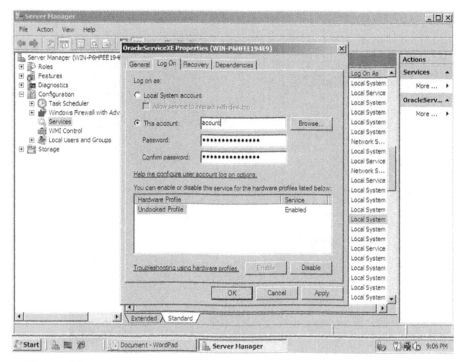

Figure 6.7: *Account Credentials Screen*

Both the *General* and *Log On* tabs within the Properties screen can be quite useful.

Now that we have covered these basics within the System Management Console, we will move on to discuss how to control Windows services using the command line. The first command we will cover is the *net* command.

Controlling Services Using the *net* Command

Windows services can also be controlled via the command line using the *net* command. The command *net start* without any arguments will list all the running services, as seen in the next screen. Note the Oracle instance service *OracleServiceXE* and the *OracleXETNSListener* services.

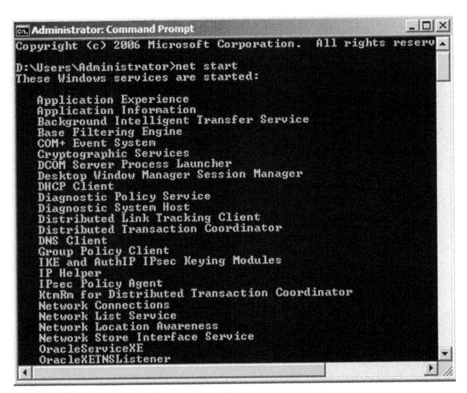

Figure 6.8: *List of Running Services*

The *net start* command followed by the service name starts the service. For example:

```
C:>net start OracleServiceXE
```

The *net stop* command followed by the service name stops the service. For example:

```
C:>net stop OracleServiceXE
```

The sequence in the following example shows stopping the Oracle service using *net stop* and starting it up using *net start*.

It also shows going into SQL*Plus and doing a *shutdown immediate*. Note that doing an Oracle shutdown does not affect the Windows service. The Windows service still runs regardless of whether the database itself is up or down. That is seen by the *net start* piped into *findstr*, still finding the service in the list of running services.

Figure 6.9: *Stopping and Starting Oracle Service*

The *sc* command can also be quite useful as it relates to Windows services. The *sc* command will be discussed next.

Controlling Services Using the *sc* Command

Windows services can also be controlled via the command line using the Service Control (*sc*) command. The *sc* command has many arguments and is quite powerful. It allows listing, starting, stopping, creating, and deleting Windows services, among other things.

Currently there are over thirty *sc* command functions, but we will focus on the most commonly used items: *query*, *queryex*, *start*, *stop*, and *delete*. Further study can be done on the rest in the many websites and Windows Server books available. The command *sc query* without any arguments lists all the running services in detail, as seen below.

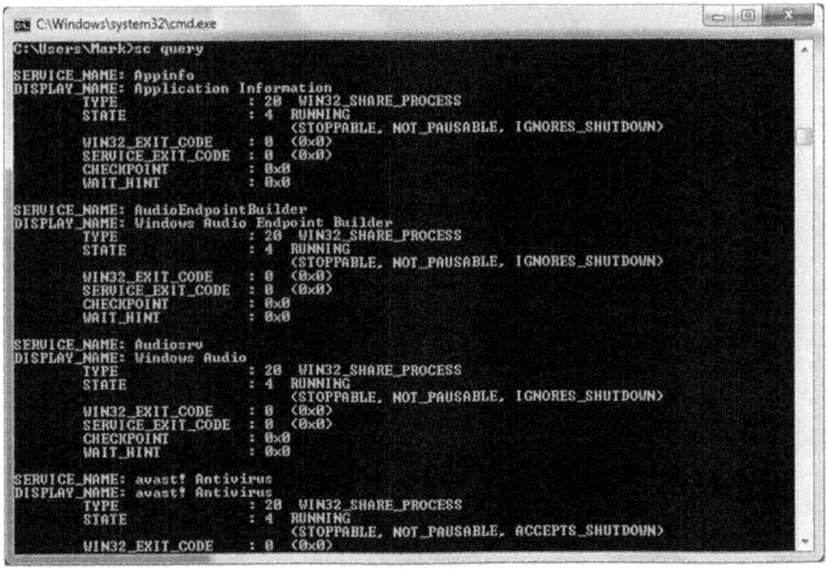

```
C:\Windows\system32\cmd.exe
C:\Users\Mark>sc query

SERVICE_NAME: Appinfo
DISPLAY_NAME: Application Information
        TYPE               : 20  WIN32_SHARE_PROCESS
        STATE              : 4  RUNNING
                                (STOPPABLE, NOT_PAUSABLE, IGNORES_SHUTDOWN)
        WIN32_EXIT_CODE    : 0  (0x0)
        SERVICE_EXIT_CODE  : 0  (0x0)
        CHECKPOINT         : 0x0
        WAIT_HINT          : 0x0

SERVICE_NAME: AudioEndpointBuilder
DISPLAY_NAME: Windows Audio Endpoint Builder
        TYPE               : 20  WIN32_SHARE_PROCESS
        STATE              : 4  RUNNING
                                (STOPPABLE, NOT_PAUSABLE, IGNORES_SHUTDOWN)
        WIN32_EXIT_CODE    : 0  (0x0)
        SERVICE_EXIT_CODE  : 0  (0x0)
        CHECKPOINT         : 0x0
        WAIT_HINT          : 0x0

SERVICE_NAME: Audiosrv
DISPLAY_NAME: Windows Audio
        TYPE               : 20  WIN32_SHARE_PROCESS
        STATE              : 4  RUNNING
                                (STOPPABLE, NOT_PAUSABLE, IGNORES_SHUTDOWN)
        WIN32_EXIT_CODE    : 0  (0x0)
        SERVICE_EXIT_CODE  : 0  (0x0)
        CHECKPOINT         : 0x0
        WAIT_HINT          : 0x0

SERVICE_NAME: avast! Antivirus
DISPLAY_NAME: avast! Antivirus
        TYPE               : 20  WIN32_SHARE_PROCESS
        STATE              : 4  RUNNING
                                (STOPPABLE, NOT_PAUSABLE, ACCEPTS_SHUTDOWN)
        WIN32_EXIT_CODE    : 0  (0x0)
```

Figure 6.10: *Result of sc query Command*

Entering the command *sc queryex* without any arguments lists all the running services in even more detail, including the Process ID, as seen in Figure 6.11.

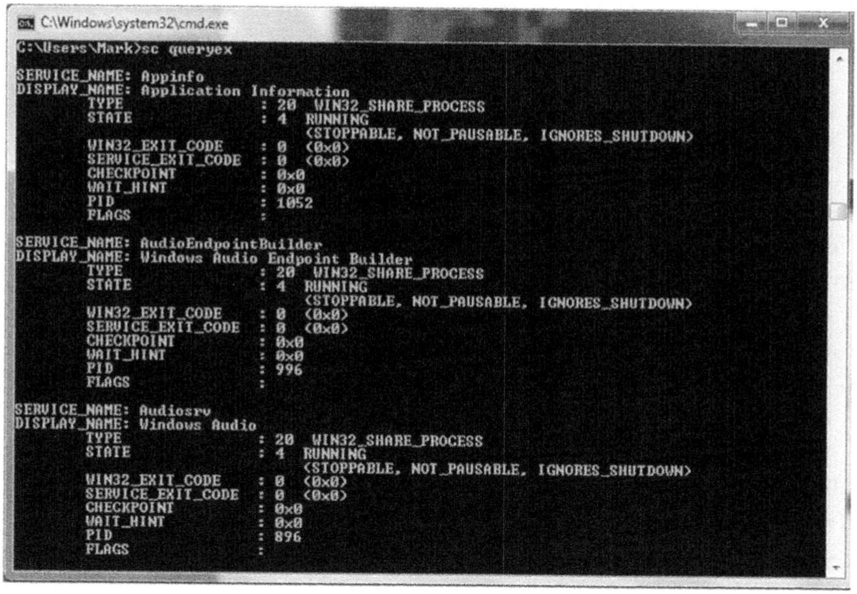

Figure 6.11: *Result of sc queryex Command*

To build upon this, either *sc query* or *sc queryex*, followed by the service name of a specific service, displays the details of that service. Getting the process ID can be useful for things such as deleting a running service that is stuck using the *taskkill* command, as will be seen in later chapters.

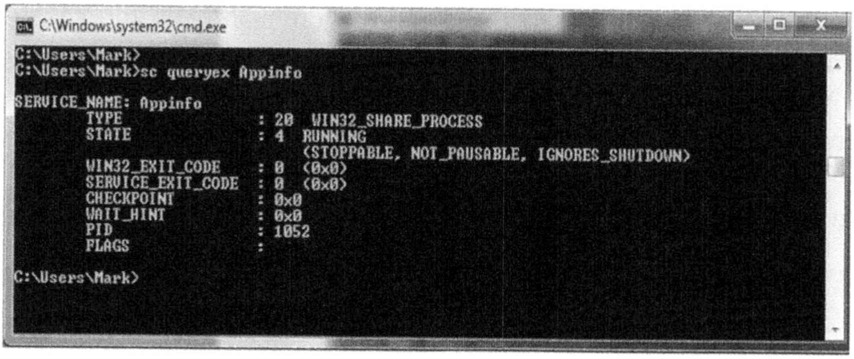

Figure 6.12: *Example of Details of a Specific Service*

Controlling Services Using the sc Command

The *sc start* command followed by the service name starts the service. For example:

```
C:>sc start OracleServiceXE
```

The *sc stop* command followed by the service name stops the service. For example:

```
C:>sc stop OracleServiceXE
```

The same rules apply for using *net stop* and *net start*, or the GUI, in that doing an Oracle shutdown does not affect the Windows service. The Windows service still runs regardless of whether the database itself is up or down.

Lastly, the *sc delete* command actually deletes the service. Be careful with this because once this is done, whichever service was deleted will need to be recreated. That may or may not be easy depending upon which one is removed!

Summary

Windows services are unique to the Windows environment and can be monitored and controlled in many ways. Controlling services via the System Management Console, the *net* command, and the *sc* command were demonstrated in this chapter.

The main points of this chapter include:

- A single Oracle service spawns a single process called *oracle.exe*, and *oracle.exe* directly controls that Oracle background processes for the instance (DBWR, SMON, PMON, etc.).

- The main function of services in Windows is to allow easy starting and stopping of the *oracle.exe* and listener services.

- There are several ways to autostart Oracle services, including service properties screen, OEM, and registry keys.

- The Oracle service can be controlled via the System Management Console, the command line using *net* commands and using the Windows *sc* command.

Now that we have covered the basics of controlling Windows services, let's move on to the basics of scheduling batch jobs in Windows.

Windows Batch Jobs

Introduction

As a review, a batch job is a non-interactive program (or set of programs) that are chained together to perform a specific task. In UNIX/Linux, batch jobs are scheduled with the *crontab* command and in Windows, batch jobs can be submitted in one of three ways and two internal ways.

External Windows batch command scheduling methods:

- **GUI interface**: The first and most obvious way is via the graphical user interface – the Windows Task Scheduler.

- **"schtasks" command line interface**: The newer *schtasks* utility is made for scheduling batch jobs.

- **"at" command line interface**: This is done at the command line level using the time tested *at* utility. The *at* command is still available for backwards compatibility, but it is no longer the preferred command line scheduling method (the *at* command will be discussed in more detail later in this chapter).

Internal Windows batch command scheduling methods:

- **dbms_scheduler**: This is a robust command line scheduler for jobs internal to Oracle. Unlike the external scheduler, the *dbms_scheduler* remembers any "missed" jobs.

- **dbms_job**: This has been deprecated, but it is still available for scheduling batch jobs in Oracle.

All of the above are useful in their own way. So, what is the point of submitting a batch job via the command line when the GUI can be used? Well, the answer is if we want to submit a batch job as part of a script, or if from within a job we want to continue to resubmit that job again until a certain condition is met, using the command line is the way to go. For static, single jobs, the Windows Task Scheduler GUI is robust enough for singleton jobs such as backups and Data Pump exports.

Batch Jobs Using the Windows Task Scheduler (Windows 2003)

To access the Windows Task Scheduler in 2003, go to:

Start → Control Panel
  mouse over *Scheduled Tasks.*

This will bring up a choice to click *Add Scheduled Task*, as shown in Figure 7.1.

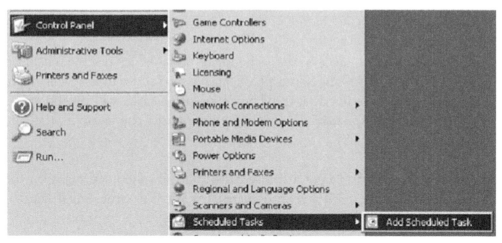

Figure 7.1: *Accessing Windows Task Scheduler - Windows 2003*

If there are already scheduled tasks on the system, they will be displayed directly below the *Add Scheduled Task* icon, as seen in the next screenshot. Note that there is an *export_orcl* task listed.

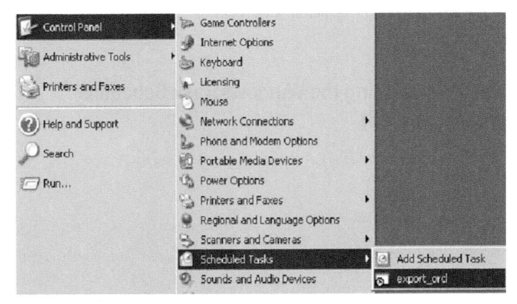

Figure 7.2: *Example of an Already Scheduled Task*

The other way to access the scheduled tasks is to double click on *Scheduled Tasks* from the same place, and a separate window will open, displaying the scheduled tasks. The status of all tasks will be shown, as well as the *Add Scheduled Task* icon, which works the same as the one above (see Figure 7.3).

This is a handy way to get a full status of all the scheduled tasks on the server at a glance. The next sequences work the same, regardless of where it is started from.

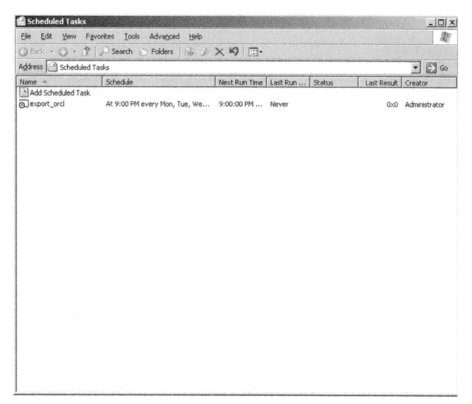

Figure 7.3: *Accessing Scheduled Tasks*

In the next sequences, creating a new Scheduled Task in Windows 2003 will be reviewed, specifically the *export_orcl* Oracle Export job as seen above.

First, navigate to the *Add Scheduled Task* icon as above and click it. This will bring up the *Scheduled Task Wizard*, as seen in Figure 7.4.

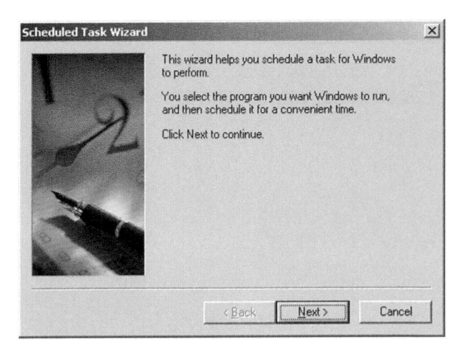

Figure 7.4: *Scheduled Task Wizard*

Click *Next* to continue and choose the application.

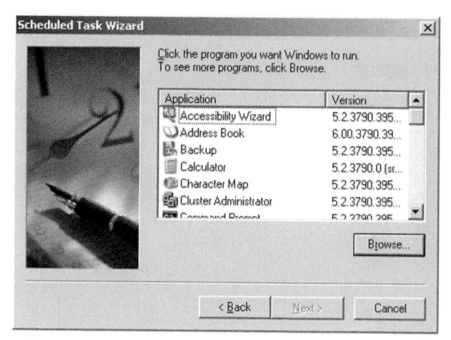

Figure 7.5: *List of Applications Available*

Click *Browse* to open the *Select Program to Schedule* screen.

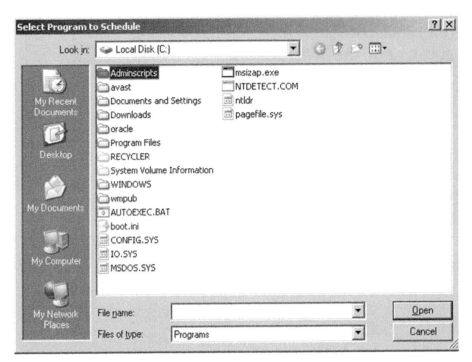

Figure 7.6: *Selecting Program to Schedule Screen*

Here, navigate to the program to execute as desired. In this example, navigate to the *C:\Adminscripts* folder.

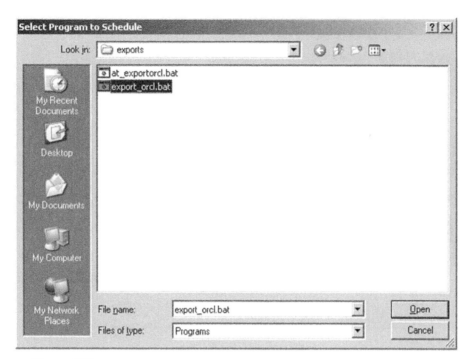

Figure 7.7: *Navigating to Selected Program*

From here, choose the exports subfolder and the *export_orcl.bat* script, and click *Open*.

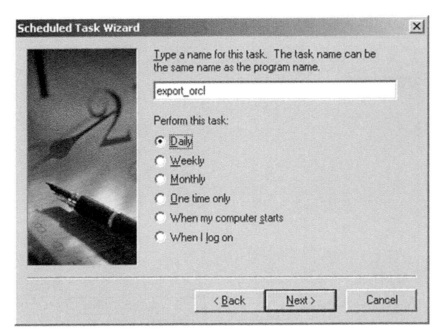

Figure 7.8: *Naming the Scheduled Task*

This screen allows for typing in a name for the job. Here, just call it the same name as the batch script, but anything can be typed here.

We also can choose the frequency of the run. For this example, *Daily* is used.

Creating naming standards for batch jobs can be important.

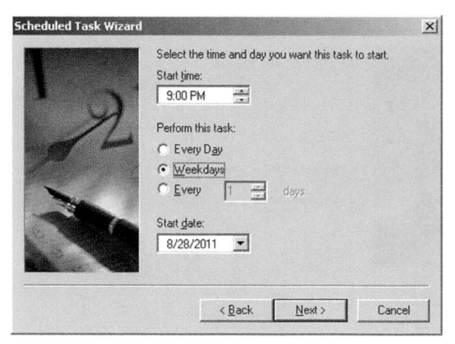

Figure 7.9: *Choosing Scheduled Task Start Time*

For the start time, 9:00 PM every weekday is chosen.

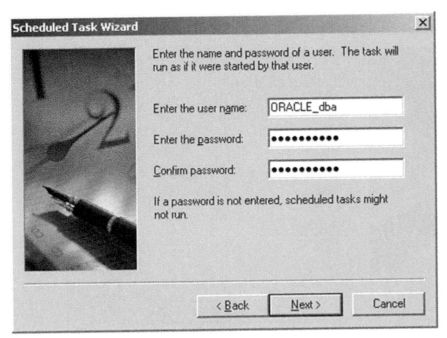

Figure 7.10: *Entering Credentials of the Windows Account*

The screen above shows the credentials of the Windows account, either *local* or *Active Directory,* for the executed task.

Be sure that this user is a member of the local group *ora_dba* if a job is being run that executes Oracle commands requiring SYS access. It is important that tasks run with the correct credentials as running tasks under privileged accounts can introduce potential security holes.

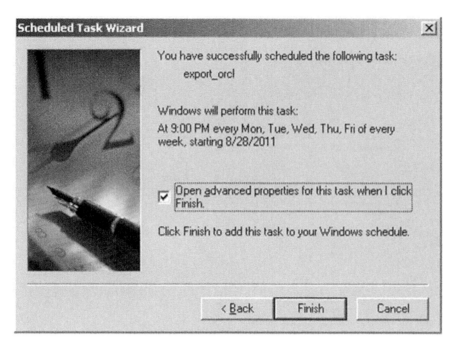

Figure 7.11: *Finishing the Scheduling of a Task*

Finally, a summary page is displayed which gives the option of displaying the advanced properties dialog once the job definition is complete.

If this option is left unchecked, the job will be submitted.

However, see the next page for a little tip that can be enacted if the checkbox is used.

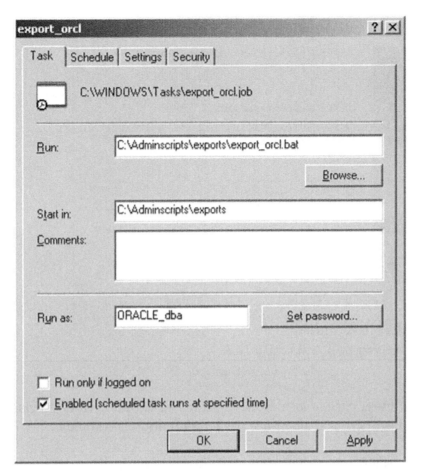

Figure 7.12: *Screen That Appears When Open Advanced Properties is Checked*

After clicking *Finish* with the *Open advanced properties* checked, the above screen displays. If having the job generate a log when it runs is desired, add a redirect in the run line in this screen as seen in Figure 7.13.

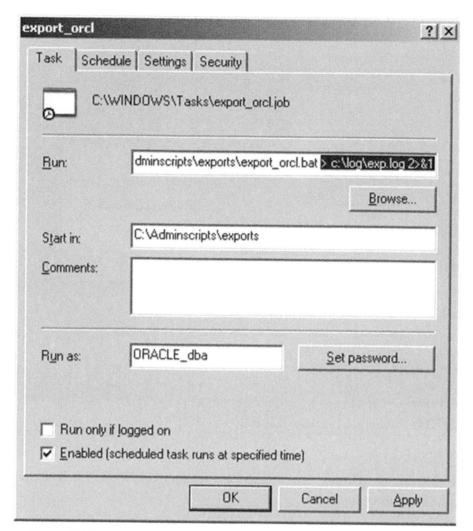

Figure 7.13: *Adding a Redirect*

Now type > *c:\log\exp.log 2>&1* (as highlighted) after the path to the script. This will log all the output to *c:\log\exp.log*. This is very handy for checking to be sure the job ran and for troubleshooting if it were to fail someplace in the middle!

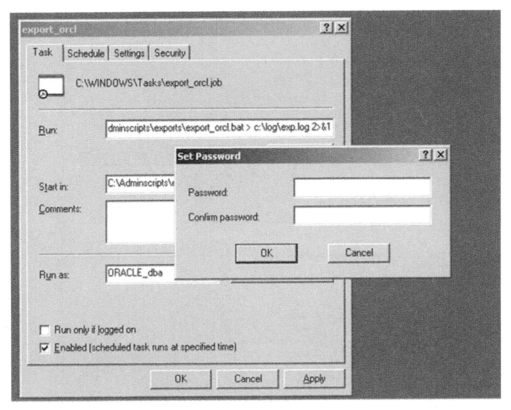

Figure 7.14: *Password Verification Request*

Once this change, or any others, has been made, the Wizard will ask for the password once again to verify.

Once entered and *OK* is clicked, then the job is submitted and can be seen in the list as shown in Figure 7.15.

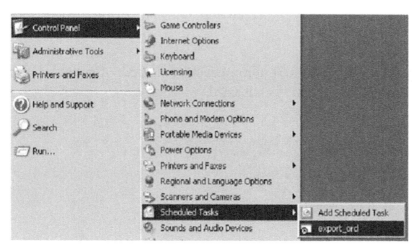

Figure 7.15: *Job Listed as Scheduled Task*

From this point, the job is scheduled and will run at the designated time and frequency. If changes need to be made, all that needs to be done is right click the displayed task and select *Properties*.

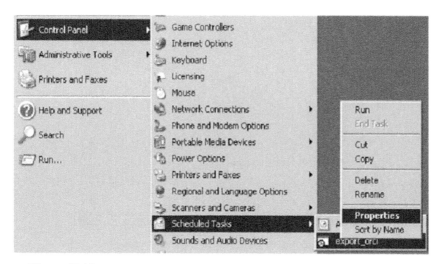

Figure 7.16: *Making Changes to Scheduled Task*

This will bring up the *Properties* screen and allow any of the properties of the job to be changed.

Note also that the job can be run immediately, deleted, or renamed using the choices listed when right click is used.

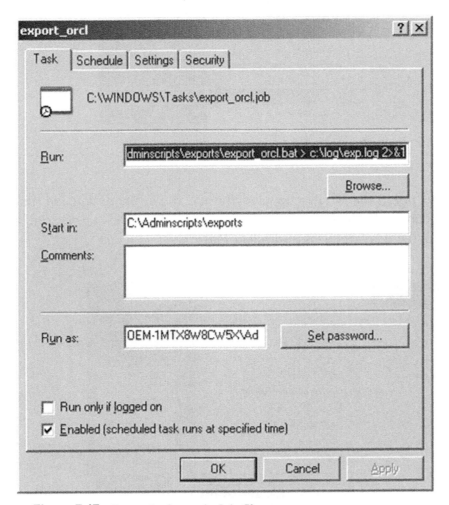

Figure 7.17: *Properties Screen for Job Changes*

The *Task*, *Schedule*, *Settings*, and *Security* can all be changed here.

One tip that can be used is in the *Advanced* screen of the *Scheduling* tab. If we want to run a specific job on a recurring basis, such as every 10 minutes, we can do that as shown next.

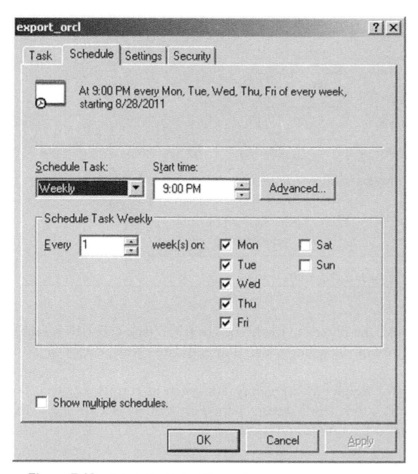

Figure 7.18: *Scheduling Tab of Properties*

First, navigate to the *Schedule* tab and click on *Advanced*. The Advanced screen appears.

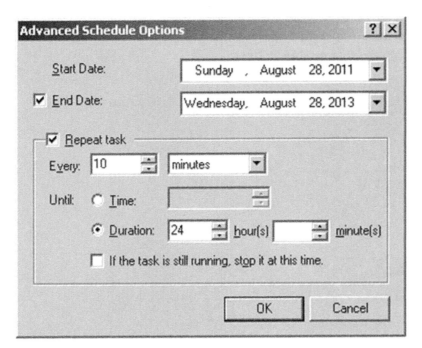

Figure 7.19: *Advanced Schedule Options*

In this example, the choice is made to repeat the task every 10 minutes for 24 hours, optionally giving a start and end date. Next, click *OK*.

This is great for frequently repeating tasks such as scripts to check the Oracle Alert Log for *ORA-* errors periodically, to check to see if the Oracle services are running, and more.

Now let's look at how batch jobs are scheduled in Windows 2008.

Batch Jobs Using the Windows Task Scheduler (Windows 2008)

To access the Windows Task Scheduler in 2008, go to:

Start → click *Administrative Tools* → click *Task Scheduler*.
This will bring up the *Task Scheduler* screen.

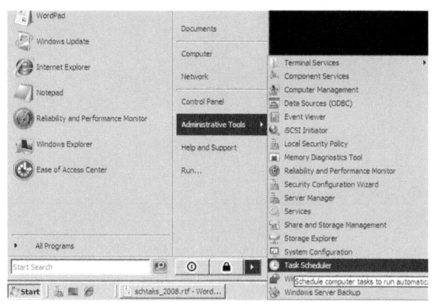

Figure 7.20: *Finding Task Scheduler in Windows 2008*

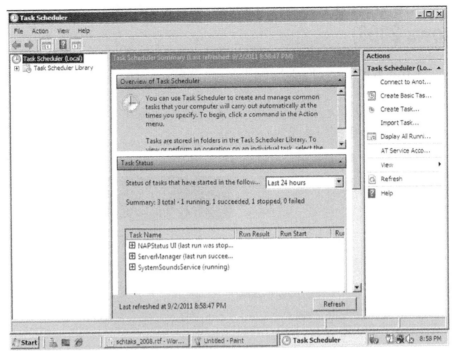

Figure 7.21: *Task Scheduler Summary*

From here, go to the left panel and expand the Task Scheduler Library.

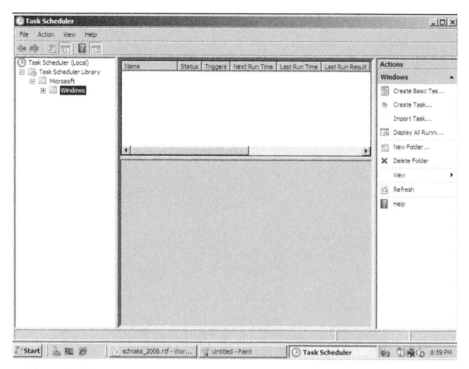

Figure 7.22: *Task Scheduler Library - Expanded*

Then navigate to the folder where the job is to be created, which is being placed in *Microsoft\Windows*. Next, move to the right panel and click *Create Task*. This will bring up the *Create Task* screen.

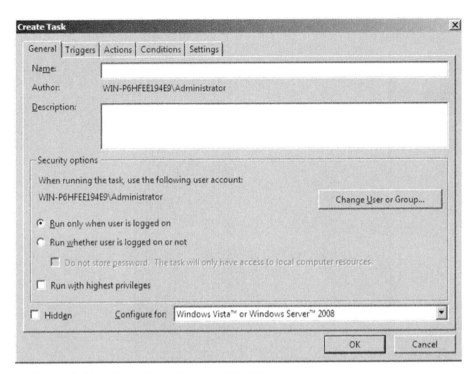

Figure 7.23: *Create Task Screen in Task Scheduler*

What appears first is the *General* tab of the *Create Task* screen.

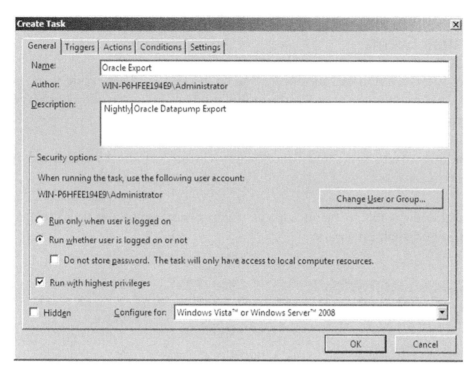

Figure 7.24: *Entering in Information in Create Task - General Screen*

This is where the batch job name is entered; in this example, Oracle Export. A description can also be put in (optional), in which the screen shows that Nightly Oracle Data Pump Export has been entered.

It is important to click the *Run whether user is logged on or not* button; otherwise, the job will only run when the user is actually logged on to the server.

It is also important to check the *Run with highest privileges* box so that the job will have the full permissions of the account it is running under.

Scheduling Windows Batch Jobs to be Triggered by System Events

The Oracle database supports system triggers, where code can be executed at database startup, shutdown, and other system-level database events.

Windows offers the same functionality on any of the events listed in Figure 7.26.

To schedule a job to begin with a system event, go to the task creation screen and click on *Triggers*.

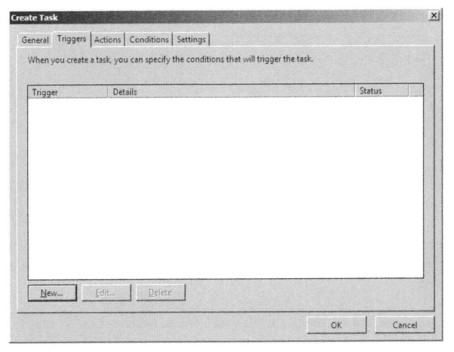

Figure 7.25: *Triggers Tab in Create Task*

The *Trigger* screen is where the schedule is set, which is accessed by clicking *New*. This will display the *New Trigger* screen as seen in Figure 7.26.

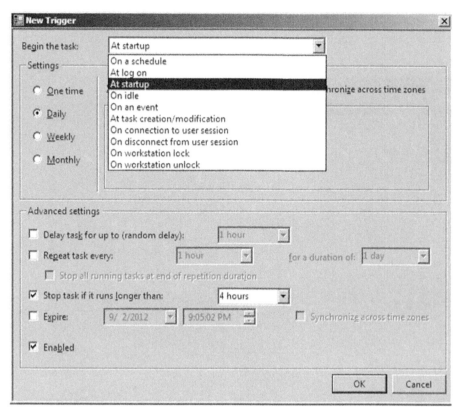

Figure 7.26: *New Trigger Screen*

Scheduling Windows Batch Jobs to be Triggered by Dates and Times

The *New Trigger* screen is where the time and date are chosen for the batch run. *On a schedule* is chosen from the *Begin the task:* dropdown at the top, as seen in Figure 7.27.

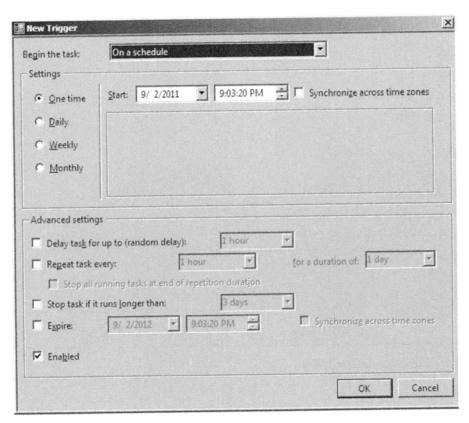

Figure 7.27: *Default Settings for New Trigger*

The default is *One time* at the current date and time.

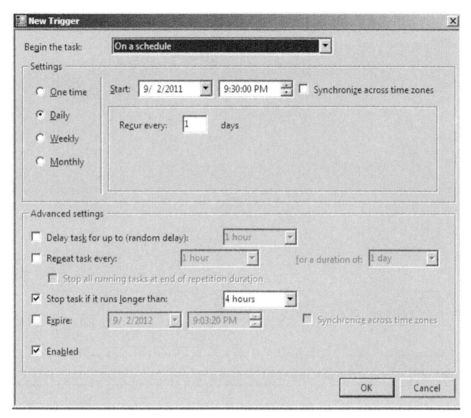

Figure 7.28: *Example of Creating New Trigger*

In this example, choose Daily at 9:30 PM, check the *Stop task if it runs longer than:* box and choose 4 hours, then check the *Enabled* box. If the *Enabled* box is not checked, the job will get created but will not run until this box gets checked.

Next, click *OK* to continue. This returns us to the main screen, where we will move on to the *Actions* tab.

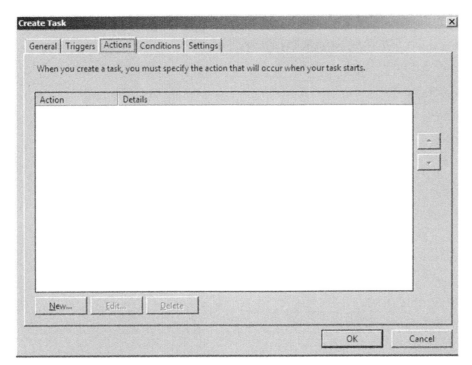

Figure 7.29: *Actions Tab in Create Task*

This screen is where the actual task to be run is selected. This is done by clicking the *New* button at the bottom left.

Windows for Oracle DBAs

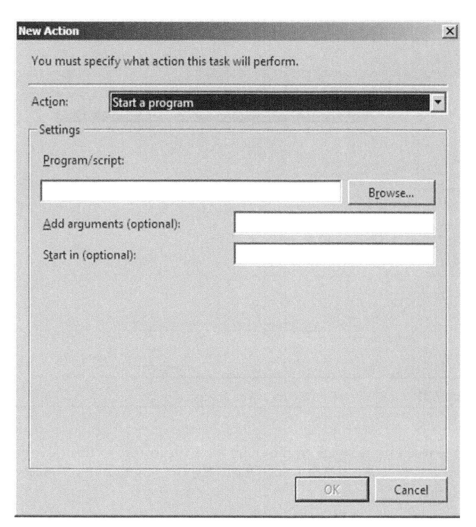

Figure 7.30: *Choosing Start a Program in New Actions*

Choose *Start a program* at the *Action* dropdown, and then click on *Browse...* to locate the script that should be run. That will take us to the browser screen.

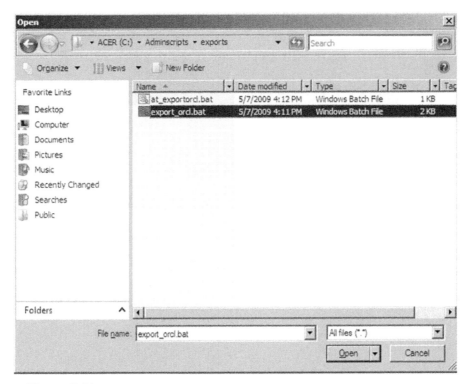

Figure 7.31: *Opened Browser Screen to Locate Script*

This is where to navigate to the script we wish to run; in this case, the *export_orcl.bat* script, which is an Oracle Export scripted in a Windows batch file.

Highlight the script name, which will place it in the *File name:* box at the bottom, and then click *Open*. This will bring us back to the *New Action* screen.

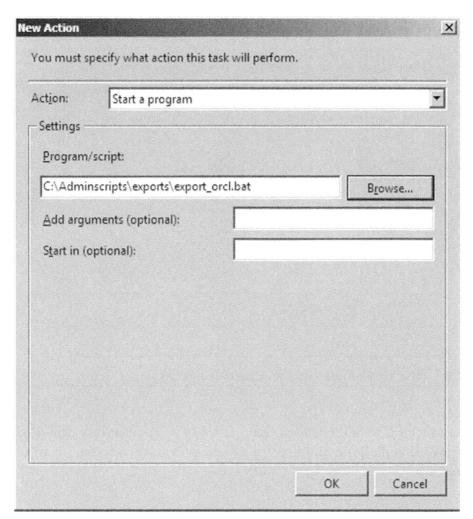

Figure 7.32: *New Action Screen with Program Selected*

Now the *Action* screen displays the name of the script/program that needs to be executed; click *OK* to accept it. This brings us back to the general *Create Task* screen.

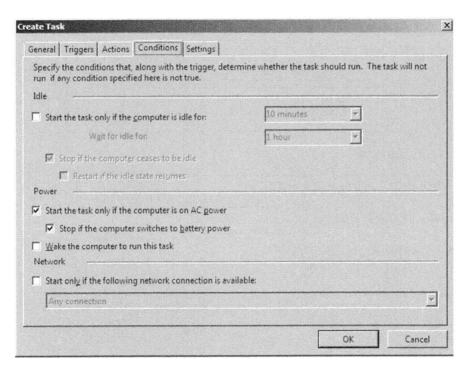

Figure 7.33: *Choosing Conditions Tab in Create Task Screen*

Now move on to the *Conditions* tab. Choose to run the task only if on AC power, and stop if running on battery power, then move on to the *Settings* tab.

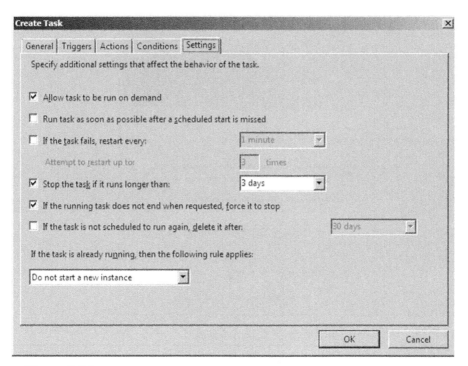

Figure 7.34: *Information in Settings Tab*

In the *Settings* tab, choose to allow the task to be run on demand, and make it stop if it runs longer than a predetermined time; the example here is 3 days, but generally state some time past when it should have always been completed. There are other options such as automatically deleting a one-time job.

Once selecting the parameters has been completed, click *OK* to submit the task.

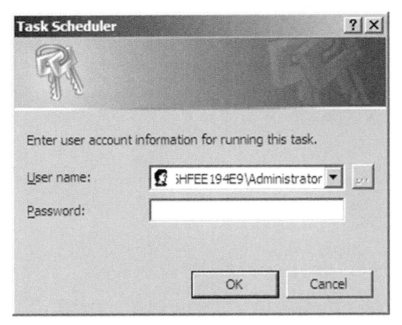

Figure 7.35: *Authentication Screen in Task Scheduler*

Once *OK* is clicked, an authentication screen is displayed.

Here is where the owner of the job (Windows User name and Password) is supplied. This user determines the system privileges for the batch job.

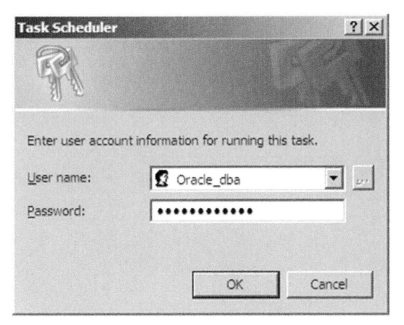

Figure 7.36: *User Name and Password Entered In*

Here we enter the *Oracle_dba* Windows service account and the password for this user. Remember that if Oracle tasks are being performed in the job that requires / *as SYSDBA* access, be sure this account is a member of the *ORA_DBA* local group on the Windows Server.

Next, click *OK* to submit the job. This brings us back to the main *Task Scheduler* screen, as shown next, and the job that was just created is displayed.

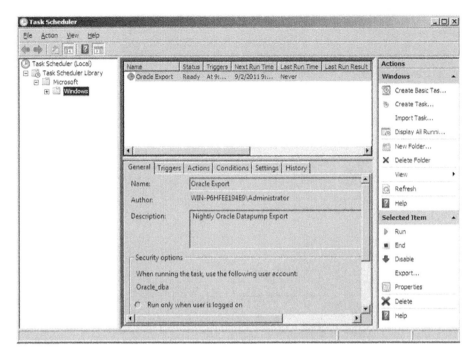

Figure 7.37: *Main Task Scheduler Screen After Job is Submitted*

Now the Task Scheduler displays the job, and the tabs immediately below show all the properties where each tab can be selected to view the settings. The properties can be edited by selecting the job in the main (center) pane, and then clicking *Properties* in the lower right panel. This will bring up the same tabs as in the display, but the settings will be changeable, as seen in the next screen.

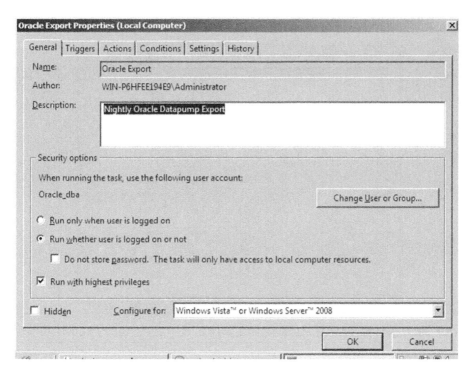

Figure 7.38: *Oracle Export Property of Selected Job*

Here, any changes can be made, and then *OK* can be selected to accept the changes or *Cancel* can be selected to cancel the changes.

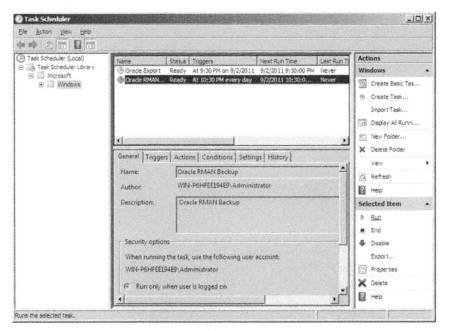

Figure 7.39: *Example with Multiple Tasks Listed*

Scrolling down in the main pane will display the properties of each job. To show how multiple tasks look in the main pane, an Oracle RMAN job has been added.

Now let's look at the most sophisticated command-line interface, the *schtasks* command for scheduling batch jobs.

Batch Jobs Using the *schtasks* Command

Now that the Task Scheduler GUI's have been thoroughly examined, there is yet more to learn. There is a command line interface to the Task Scheduler that is available in both Windows 2003 and 2008. That interface is called *schtasks*.

The *schtasks* command was introduced in Windows XP and Windows 2003 as a more flexible and slightly more verbose replacement for the *at* command. The *schtasks* command allows complete control of Windows Scheduled Tasks via the command line. This is very handy for both online work and scripting.

As with Windows 2000, the simplest way to schedule jobs in Windows XP and Windows 2003 is via the Scheduled Tasks Wizard. However, the *schtasks* command provides a command line API for situations in which a command line approach is preferable. There are several options to the *schtasks* command. A summary can be seen by typing *schtasks /?* as in Figure 7.40.

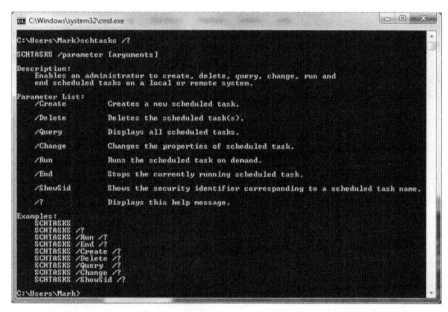

Figure 7.40: *Summary of schtasks Command Options*

The most useful options of the *schtasks* command will be reviewed now.

First, simply typing *schtasks* with no arguments will display all the currently submitted batch jobs on the system, as seen in Figure 7.41. Notice that the Oracle Export and Oracle RMAN Backup tasks that we submitted in the GUI appear, but also there are several more system level tasks displayed below those.

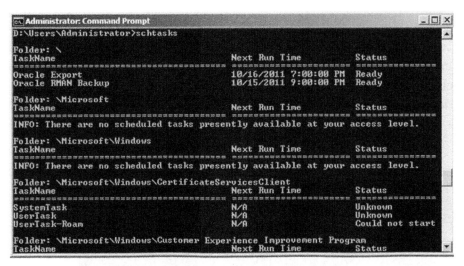

Figure 7.41: *Results of Schtasks Command with No Arguments*

The command *schtasks/query* does the same, and if the */tn* qualifier (for task name) is added, then a specific job is displayed. In the following example, the Oracle Export task is being queried.

Figure 7.42: *Querying Oracle Export Task*

Another useful switch is the */change* switch. In the example in the following pane, the start time is being changed using the command:

```
schtasks /change /tn "Oracle Export" /change /st 23:00.
```

This changes the start time to 11:00 PM. Note the query before and after to show the change has been successfully made. Most of the job parameters can be changed in this fashion; the command *schtasks /change /?* gives all of the options.

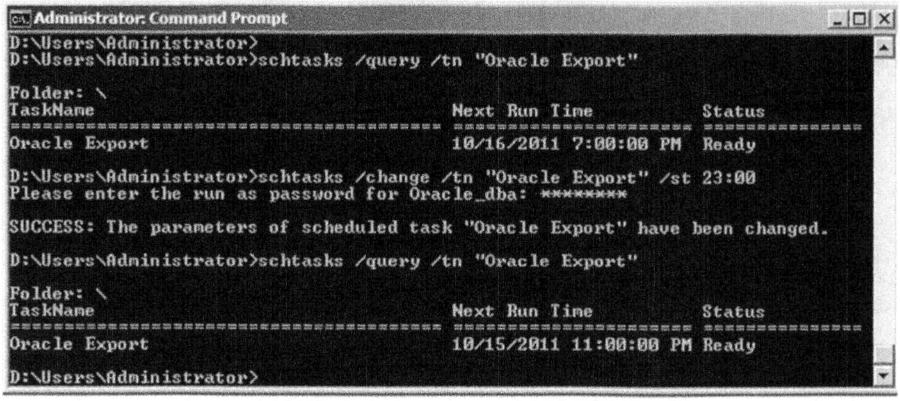

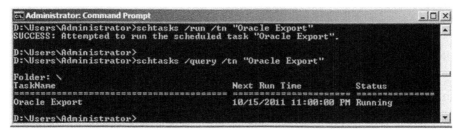

Figure 7.43: *Acknowledgement That Task Has Been Changed*

To run an existing job on demand, simply add the */run* switch. The next screen shows that the Oracle Export job is run; it is scheduled for 11:00 PM, but we are running now in real time. Note the status is *running* when queried.

Figure 7.44: *Current Status of Oracle Export Job*

Conversely, a running task can be stopped with the *end* switch. Here, a status of Ready on the subsequent query is revealed showing that the job has been stopped successfully.

Figure 7.45: *Oracle Export Job Currently Stopped*

The scheduled task can also be deleted using *schtasks /delete* followed by the task name, as shown in the pane below. The query immediately after shows that the scheduled task has been deleted.

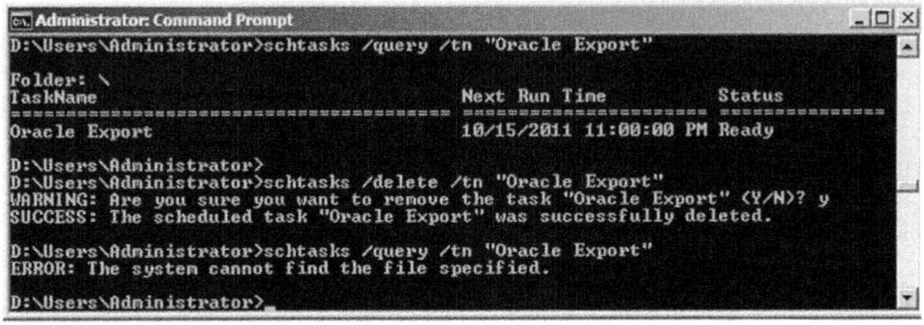

Figure 7.46: *Oracle Export Job Shown as Deleted*

Finally, if typing is preferred instead of using the GUI, or a script is being used, then a scheduled task can be created using the *schtasks /create* command. The following screen shows recreating the Oracle Export task that was just deleted.

Figure 7.47: *Recreating Oracle Export Job*

Basically, almost anything that would need to be done via the GUI can be accomplished via the command line using *schtasks*.

Let's continue our discussion of scheduling with the elderly but functional *at* command.

Batch Jobs Using the *at* Command

Windows batch jobs can be submitted and deleted via the command line using the *at* command. The *at* command can be used to schedule commands and programs on Windows NT, Windows 2000, Windows XP and Windows 2003. This is the oldest way to submit jobs and predates the Task Manager, but *at* still exists and can be used. It is quite useful for submitting a job from inside a job or for allowing a job to resubmit itself. Not nearly as robust as *schtasks*, *at* allows batch runs to be submitted and deleted from the command line.

The *at* command with no arguments displays a list of jobs submitted via *at*. It does not display tasks that are in the Task Manager. The sequence shows *at* to list the jobs, which returns none. Next, submit the *export_orcl.bat* job to run every weekday at 8:00 PM, and do another *at* to list the resultant job.

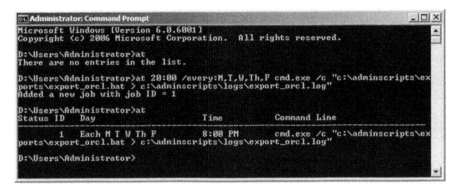

Figure 7.48: *Example of Using the at Command*

There are several things going on in the above screen. One shows the general syntax of *at*, which is:

```
at <starttime> /every:<day of week> <path to batch script>
```

The bonus here is showing how to log the output to a file. The addition of *cmd.exe /c "<bat file > log file* tells the *at* scheduler to execute the script and log output to the logfile.

Each job gets assigned a status ID. This one is first, so it is 1. A second is now created, the RMAN backup, which will get 2.

Figure 7.49: *Assigning Status IDs to Jobs*

The Status ID is useful for deleting an *at* batch job. The command is simply:

```
at <Status ID> /delete
```

In the example below, delete the export job:

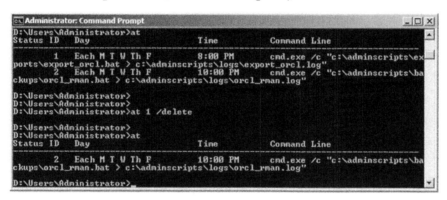

Figure 7.50: *Export Job Being Deleted*

Lastly, note that *at* does not display scheduled tasks, but *schtasks* displays and controls *at* jobs as well as scheduled tasks.

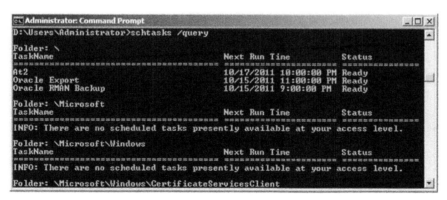

Figure 7.51: *Showing That at Does Not Display Scheduled Tasks*

More About the *at* Command

For the *at* command to work, the scheduler service must be running. On Windows, this can be done using the services dialog or from the command line using the *net* command:

```
net stop "Task Scheduler"

net start "Task Scheduler"
```

The *at /?* command produces the following:

```
AT [\\computername] [ [id] [/DELETE] | /DELETE [/YES]]

AT [\\computername] time [/INTERACTIVE]
    [ /EVERY:date[,...] | /NEXT:date[,...]] "command"

\\computername    Specifies a remote computer. Commands are
                  scheduled on the local computer if this parameter
                  is omitted.

id                Is an identification number assigned to a
                  scheduled command.

/delete           Cancels a scheduled command. If id is omitted,
                  all the scheduled commands are canceled.

/yes              Used with cancel all jobs command when no further
                  confirmation is desired.

time              Specifies the time when command is to run.

/interactive      Allows the job to interact with the desktop of
                  the user who is logged on when the job runs.

/every:date[,...] Runs the command on each specified day(s) of the
                  week or month. If date is omitted, the current
                  day of the month is assumed.

/next:date[,...]  Runs the specified command on the next occurrence
                  of the day (for example, next Thursday).  If date
                  is omitted, the current day of the month is
                  assumed.

"command"         Is the Windows NT command, or batch program to be
                  run.
```

A couple of simple examples of its use include:

```
C:> at 21:00 /every:m,t,th,f "c:\jobs\MyJob.bat"
Added a new job with job ID = 1

C:> at 6:00 /next:20 "c:\jobs\MyJob.bat"
Added a new job with job ID = 2
```

The first example schedules a job which runs the *c:\jobs\MyJob.bat* script at 9:00 PM on Mondays, Tuesdays, Thursdays and Fridays. The second example schedules a job that runs the script at 6:00 AM on the next 20th of the month.

The current list of jobs can be displayed by issuing the *at* command with no parameters:

```
C:\>at
Status ID   Day                      Time          Command Line
-----------------------------------------------------------------
         1  Each M T Th F            21:00 PM      c:\jobs\MyJob.bat
         2  Next 20                  06:00 AM      c:\jobs\MyJob.bat

C:\>
```

Jobs can be deleted using the */delete* option:

```
C:\>at 1 /delete

C:\>at 2 /delete

C:\>at
There are no entries in the list.
```

The *at* scheduler has been at the heart of Windows scheduling for some years, but recent Windows versions have introduced simpler and more flexible alternatives. The Windows Scheduler can be programmed to run Oracle Windows batch scripts either from the Windows Control Panel interface or via command line execution using the *at* command.

The Windows Scheduler needs to know three basic facts in order to run an Oracle job:

1. **Time:** The time of day to run (military HH:MM) the Windows job.

2. **Date:** The day to run the Windows job, either the day of week (M,T,W,Th,F,S,Su) or day of month (1-31) with multiple values separated by commas.

3. **Job name:** What Windows job to run.

Here are more examples of *at* scheduling of Windows jobs:

```
@echo off

REM +-------------------------------------------------
REM | Set up client specific variables
REM +-------------------------------------------------

set BC_DIR=C:\BC

REM +-------------------------------------------------
REM | Schedule BAT jobs to run at appropriate
REM | times.
REM |                   ** Caution **
REM |  The following /delete switch clears all
REM |  jobs from the Windows Scheduler
REM +-------------------------------------------------

AT /delete /yes

REM +-------------------------------------------------
REM | Schedule Monday Table & Index Reports
REM +-------------------------------------------------

AT  6:30 /every:M  cmd /c %BC_DIR%\script\get_obj_stats.bat
AT  7:30 /every:M  cmd /c %BC_DIR%\script\weekly_rpt_dba.bat
AT  7:40 /every:M  cmd /c %BC_DIR%\script\weekly_rpt_mgt.bat

REM +-------------------------------------------------
REM | A daily STATSPACK alert
REM +-------------------------------------------------

AT  7:00 /every:M,T,W,Th,F,S,Su cmd /c
%BC_DIR%\script\statspack_alert_9i.bat

REM +-------------------------------------------------
REM | Disk Free Space Alert every 6 hours
REM +-------------------------------------------------

AT  6:30 /every:M,T,W,Th,F,S,Su  cmd /c %BC_DIR%\script\disk_space.bat
AT 12:30 /every:M,T,W,Th,F,S,Su  cmd /c %BC_DIR%\script\disk_space.bat
AT 18:30 /every:M,T,W,Th,F,S,Su  cmd /c %BC_DIR%\script\disk_space.bat
AT 00:30 /every:M,T,W,Th,F,S,Su  cmd /c %BC_DIR%\script\disk_space.bat
```

```
REM +--------------------------------------------------
REM | Schedule a Monday STATSPACK snapshot removal
REM +--------------------------------------------------

AT  7:45 /every:M  cmd /c %BC_DIR%\script\sprem.bat

REM +--------------------------------------------------
REM | Schedule a periodic Trace File alert
REM +--------------------------------------------------

AT  0:00 /every:M,T,W,Th,F,S,Su  cmd /c %BC_DIR%\script\trace_alert.bat
AT  6:00 /every:M,T,W,Th,F,S,Su  cmd /c %BC_DIR%\script\trace_alert.bat
AT 12:00 /every:M,T,W,Th,F,S,Su  cmd /c %BC_DIR%\script\trace_alert.bat
AT 18:00 /every:M,T,W,Th,F,S,Su  cmd /c %BC_DIR%\script\trace_alert.bat

REM +--------------------------------------------------
REM | Schedule a daily Alert Log check
REM +--------------------------------------------------

AT  7:15 /every:M,T,W,Th,F,S,Su cmd /c %BC_DIR%\script\alert_log.bat
```

Now that we've seen how to schedule jobs using the *at* command, we will move on to Oracle Internal job scheduling.

Oracle Internal Job Scheduling

Within Oracle, scheduling jobs can be done using the *dbms_job* and *dbms_scheduler* packages. In Windows, this can be done by invoking SQL*Plus in a *bat* file. The trick is to put the whole *sqlplus* command on a single line:

```
c:> type run_oracle.bat

@echo OFF
set MYDIR=C:\oracle\scripts
sqlplus -s fred/flintstone @%MYDIR%\rpt_dba.sql
exit
```

It is important to note that you can only have one file argument to SQL*Plus in Windows.

For example, this command will fail because two SQL files are specified:

```
sqlplus "/as sysdba" @C:\Users\Test\1.sql @C:\Users\Test\2.sql
```

You can execute many SQL scripts and commands in Windows SQL*Plus by using this technique, using the *type* command to paste together all of the commands:

```
type C:\Users\Test\1.sql > c:\temp\runme.sql

type C:\Users\Test\2.sql >> c:\temp\runme.sql

sqlplus "/as sysdba" @C:\temp\runme.sql
```

Again, Oracle provides a great alternative to external Windows scheduling with the *at* command, using Oracle's own internal scheduler. This can be invoked via Oracle Enterprise Manager (OEM), but most Windows batch files use the *dbms_scheduler* package.

There is an excellent overview of Oracle shell scripting best practices in book "Oracle Shell Scripting" by Jon Emmons, and see the book "Oracle Job Scheduling" for an overview of using *dbms_scheduler* for executing external shell scripts within Oracle.

Oracle's *dbms_scheduler* package makes it possible to "shell-out" to the OS environment, executing shell scripts and *bat* files, directly from within Oracle.

Also, note that it's possible to embed OS commands directly inside PL/SQL.

The following working script invokes a Windows *bat* file from inside Oracle, using the *dbms_scheduler* syntax:

```
begin dbms_scheduler.drop_job (job_name=>'daily_backup'); end;
/
begin  dbms_scheduler.drop_program(program_name    => 'backup_database');
end;
/
begin  dbms_scheduler.drop_schedule(schedule_name =>
'daily_at_4am_except_monday'); end;
/

begin
```

```
  dbms_scheduler.create_schedule(
      schedule_name    => 'daily_at_4am_except_monday',
      repeat_interval  => 'FREQ=DAILY; INTERVAL=1;
BYDAY=TUE,WED,THU,FRI,SAT,SUN; BYHOUR=4',
      comments         => 'schedule to run daily at 4am except on mondays');
  dbms_scheduler.create_program
    ( program_name    => 'backup_database',
      program_type    => 'EXECUTABLE',
      program_action  => 'd:\oracle\product\admin\dw\scripts\backup_dw.bat >
nul',
      enabled         => TRUE,
      comments        => 'Backup dw database using rman and then backup rman
database via hot backup.'
    );

  dbms_scheduler.create_job (
    job_name=>'daily_backup',
    program_name =>'backup_database',
      schedule_name=> 'DAILY_AT_4AM_EXCEPT_MONDAY',
    enabled         => true,
      comments        => 'backs up the dw and rman databases daily at 4am
except on for mondays.'
  );
end; /

select * from dba_scheduler_jobs
```

Summary

This chapter was an introduction to Oracle batch job scheduling, and reviewed the three external (GUI, *schtasks* and the *at* command) and internal commands (the *dbms_scheduler* and *dbms_job*).

The main points of this chapter include:

- Batch jobs/scheduled tasks can be submitted and controlled via the GUI in both Windows 2003 and 2008 and can also be controlled on the command line using *schtasks*.

- For command line utilities, we see the *schtasks* command.

- The *at* command is the granddaddy of batch commands and has limited functionality.

- The best way to learn how these job scheduling tasks operate is to try them!

Now that we see the basics of scheduling batch jobs in Windows, let's move on and look at network commands in Windows.

Network Commands on Windows

Introduction

In Windows Server, we have several options at the command prompt for network commands. This chapter will provide a brief overview of these network commands.

We will limit the discussion of networking commands to a few that I have found to be the most useful. There are many others, and any good book on Windows or an Internet search will give you plenty of detailed information on them.

The networking commands we will review are:

- *Ipconfig*
- *Ping*
- *Nslookup*
- *Tracert*

We will also review how to connect to disks on remote servers. Let's begin by taking a look at the *ipconfig* command.

Using *ipconfig* to get your TCP/IP Address

The simplest way to get your general information, such as TCP/IP address, default gateway, and subnet mask, is with the *ipconfig* command. This may be needed for networking, checking connectivity, or for things such as software licensing. The output looks like Figure 8.1.

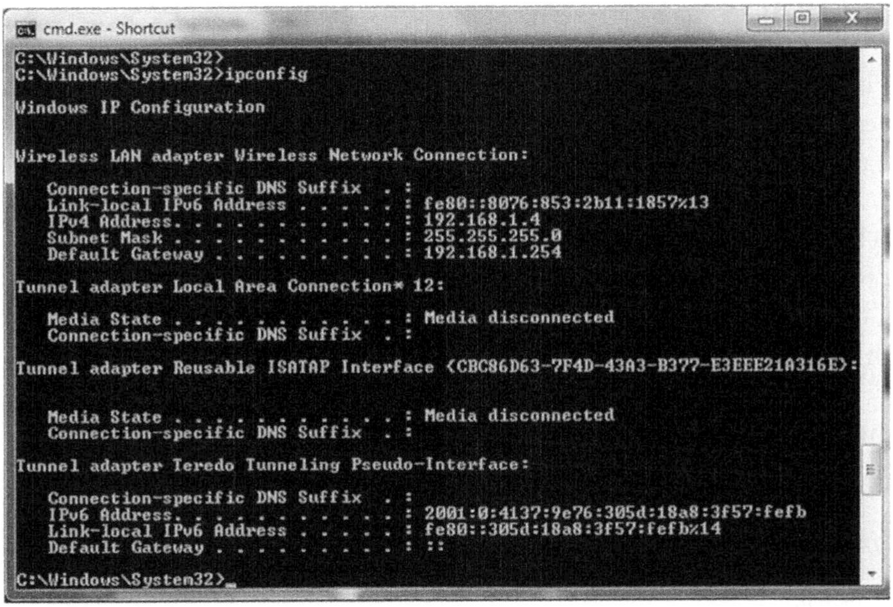

Figure 8.1: *ipconfig Command Output*

Windows 2003 and 2008 work the same way. Note that both the IPv4 and IPv6 addresses are shown at the top, as well as default gateway and subnet mask.

Next, let's see how the *netstat –an* command can be used to see which ports the server is listening on.

Using the *netstat –an* Command

The *netstat –an* command can be used to see which network ports the server is listening on. This can be further modified by piping to the *find* command to see only TCP ports, if desired, as seen in Figure 8.2. Note that port 1521 is being listened on, indicating that the Oracle listener is running.

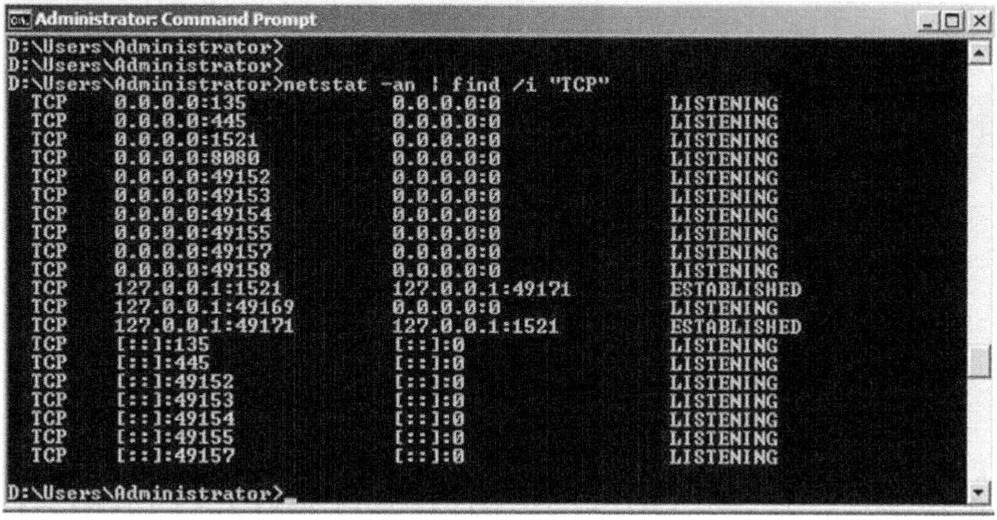

```
Administrator: Command Prompt                                            _ □ ×
D:\Users\Administrator>
D:\Users\Administrator>
D:\Users\Administrator>netstat -an | find /i "TCP"
  TCP    0.0.0.0:135           0.0.0.0:0              LISTENING
  TCP    0.0.0.0:445           0.0.0.0:0              LISTENING
  TCP    0.0.0.0:1521          0.0.0.0:0              LISTENING
  TCP    0.0.0.0:8080          0.0.0.0:0              LISTENING
  TCP    0.0.0.0:49152         0.0.0.0:0              LISTENING
  TCP    0.0.0.0:49153         0.0.0.0:0              LISTENING
  TCP    0.0.0.0:49154         0.0.0.0:0              LISTENING
  TCP    0.0.0.0:49155         0.0.0.0:0              LISTENING
  TCP    0.0.0.0:49157         0.0.0.0:0              LISTENING
  TCP    0.0.0.0:49158         0.0.0.0:0              LISTENING
  TCP    127.0.0.1:1521        127.0.0.1:49171        ESTABLISHED
  TCP    127.0.0.1:49169       0.0.0.0:0              LISTENING
  TCP    127.0.0.1:49171       127.0.0.1:1521         ESTABLISHED
  TCP    [::]:135              [::]:0                 LISTENING
  TCP    [::]:445              [::]:0                 LISTENING
  TCP    [::]:49152            [::]:0                 LISTENING
  TCP    [::]:49153            [::]:0                 LISTENING
  TCP    [::]:49154            [::]:0                 LISTENING
  TCP    [::]:49155            [::]:0                 LISTENING
  TCP    [::]:49157            [::]:0                 LISTENING

D:\Users\Administrator>
```

Figure 8.2: *Displaying TCP Ports*

Now that we see how to view which ports the server is listening on, let's examine how to see if a server is alive and responding using *ping*.

Using *ping* to see if a Server is Responding

The simplest way to see if a server is up and responding from another server is to *ping* it. You can use either the TCP/IP address or the DNS node name as an argument. If the target machine is responding, it will reply with the address and how long it took to get a response, as shown in Figure 8.3. This can be very handy.

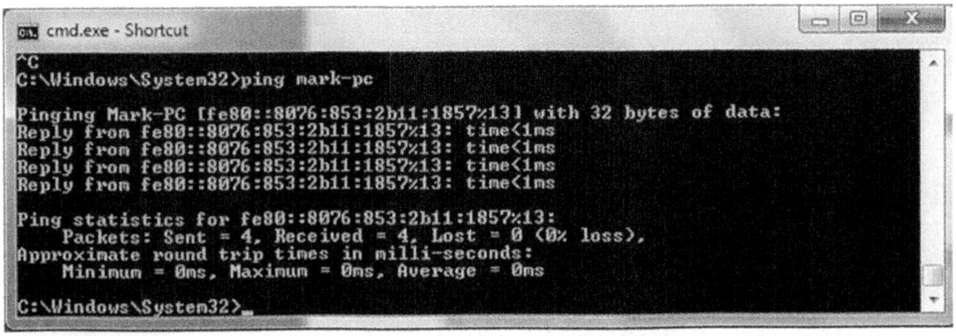

```
cmd.exe - Shortcut

^C
C:\Windows\System32>ping mark-pc

Pinging Mark-PC [fe80::8076:853:2b11:1857%13] with 32 bytes of data:
Reply from fe80::8076:853:2b11:1857%13: time<1ms
Reply from fe80::8076:853:2b11:1857%13: time<1ms
Reply from fe80::8076:853:2b11:1857%13: time<1ms
Reply from fe80::8076:853:2b11:1857%13: time<1ms

Ping statistics for fe80::8076:853:2b11:1857%13:
    Packets: Sent = 4, Received = 4, Lost = 0 (0% loss),
Approximate round trip times in milli-seconds:
    Minimum = 0ms, Maximum = 0ms, Average = 0ms

C:\Windows\System32>_
```

Figure 8.3: *Using the ping Command*

Ping can also be used as a crude network troubleshooter. If you are seeing long reply times and/or dropped (lost) packets, it is indicative of a connectivity problem.

Next, let's take a brief look at the *nslookup* command.

Using *nslookup* to get the TCP/IP Address

The *nslookup* command can be used to discover the TCP/IP address of a server. All one needs to do is follow the command with the destination dns name, fully or partially qualified, as seen in Figure 8.4.

Figure 8.4: *Using the nslookup Command*

Ping can also discover the TCP/IP address of a server, but doing so will also send test packets out.

The *tracert* command will be covered next.

Using *tracert* to get the Path/Route Server

The *tracert* command can be used to track the path a network connection takes to reach the destination, and how long each section (hop) takes. This allows us to see if there is a bottleneck someplace in our network.

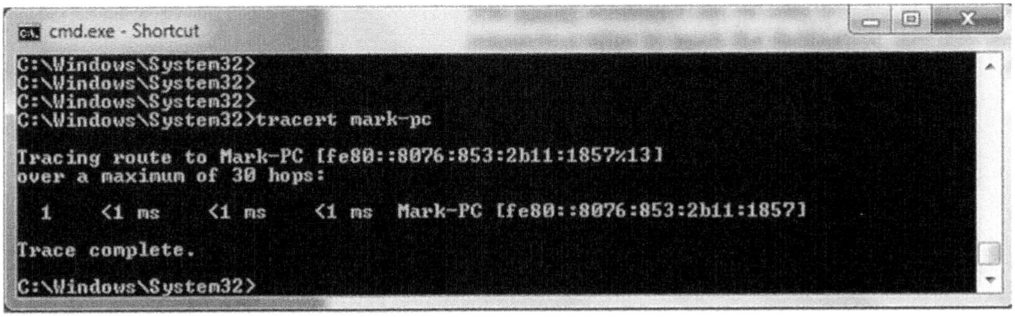

Figure 8.5: *Using the tracert Command*

Now let's take a look at connecting to another Windows Server.

Connecting to a Device on a Remote Server

At times it is handy to connect to another Windows Server to pull files from one place to another. For example, suppose you want to refresh a database and you need to copy the export file from one server to another. The following trick works IF you have permissions on the other box AND if admin shares are enabled.

To connect to a drive on another server, we simply put the UNC path to the administrative share in the *run* command.

Go to *Start*, then *Run* and type *server_name**driveletter$*

For example:

Start\run: *mark-pc**c$*

Figure 8.6: *Connecting to a Device on a Remote Server*

A Windows Explorer window will pop up connected to the C: drive from the machine mark-pc. You can then copy and paste in either direction, provided you have permissions to do so.

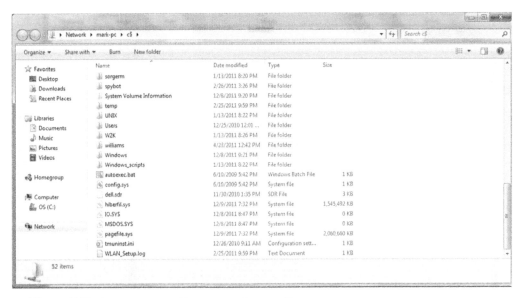

Figure 8.7: *Connecting to a Device on a Remote Server*

Finally, let's take a look at the *hostname* command.

The *hostname* Command

A handy way to see what the name of the machine you are currently using is to use the *hostname* command. Quite simply, it returns the name of the computer – as seen in Figure 8.8 below.

Figure 8.8: *Using the hostname Command*

A Word About IIS and FTP

The FTP client on Windows (outbound) from your server works by default from the command prompt. However, if you want to FTP *to* your server, you will need to install Microsoft IIS (Internet Information Services), and specify the FTP service. The FTP service does not get installed by default in the Windows Server 2003/2008 IIS Installation; you must specifically install that piece.

Summary

This chapter provided a brief introduction to a few handy command line tools that can assist with basic network-related tasks, including the use of the *ipconfig*, *netstat –an*, *nslookup*, *tracert*, and *hostname* commands.

The main points of this chapter include:

- The *ipconfig* command is the simplest way to get your TCP/IP address, default gateway, and subnet mask.

- The *netstat –an* command can find which network ports the server is listening on, and the addition of the *find* command will display only TCP ports.

- You can use *ping* to see if a server is up and responding.

- You can use the *nslookup* command to discover the TCP/IP address of a server.

- The *tracert* command can be used to track the path a network connection takes, allowing you to see if there is a bottleneck in the network.

- You can use the *hostname* command to display the name of the machine you are currently using.

While entire books have been written on these tools, including all the switches and possible uses, this chapter just touched on their most basic and everyday uses.

Now let's move on to examine killing processes in Windows.

Killing Windows Processes

A Time to Kill

There are times when an Oracle Windows program needs to die, and there are several common states where you may want to kill a program:

- **Zombie process:** The process is not consuming any computing resources and is not waiting on any system event to proceed. Zombies can sometime be left over after you bounce your Oracle database, existing as a process in Windows but having no corresponding Oracle process equivalent.

- **Runaway process:** The process is stuck in a loop, consuming huge amounts of CPU and/or RAM resources.

- **Hung process:** A hung process is consuming resources (e.g. locks) and it's stopped, waiting for a latch or lock to be released.

- **Orphaned process:** An orphan is a process where the SQL*Net client PC has disconnected from the Windows Server connection and the process waits needlessly, hoping for the connection to be re-connected.

When killing sessions and processes, we have to detect if the Windows process has a corresponding Oracle process. This is done by running the following script from within SQL*Plus.

🖫 **display_processes.sql**

```
ttitle "dbname Database|UNIX/Oracle Sessions";

set heading off;
select 'Sessions on database '||substr(name,1,8) from v$database;
set heading on;

select
   substr(a.spid,1,9) pid,
```

```
     substr(b.sid,1,5) sid,
     substr(b.serial#,1,5) ser#,
     substr(b.machine,1,6) box,
     substr(b.username,1,10) username,
     -- b.server,
     substr(b.osuser,1,8) os_user,
     substr(b.program,1,30) program
from
     v$session b,
     v$process a
where
     b.paddr = a.addr
and
     type='USER'
order by
     spid;

ttitle off;
set heading off;
select 'To kill, enter SQLPLUS> ALTER SYSTEM KILL SESSION',
''''||'SID, SER#'||''''||';' from dual;
```

If the process IDs (called "PID") do not match the Windows processes, then you may need to kill the Windows process.

In Windows Server, we have several options for killing processes. In UNIX, we can simply issue a *kill -9* to kill a running process. In Windows, it is not always that straightforward!

We have the ability to use several methods to kill a process, and many will depend on the circumstances. For example, we can use the Task Manager for jobs we have direct permissions on, and then use the Task Manager called by the *at* command to kill any others. We can also kill a process from the command line using the *taskkill* command. Lastly, we can delete a stuck Windows service by finding the process ID using the *sc queryex* and then using *taskkill*. This chapter will explore each of these methods for killing processes, beginning with the Task Manager.

Using the Task Manager to Kill a Process

The simplest way to delete a process is by using the Task Manager. In the example, seen in Figure 9.1, the *cmd.exe* process is highlighted and then *End Process* is clicked. That will kill the process, as long as we have permissions to it.

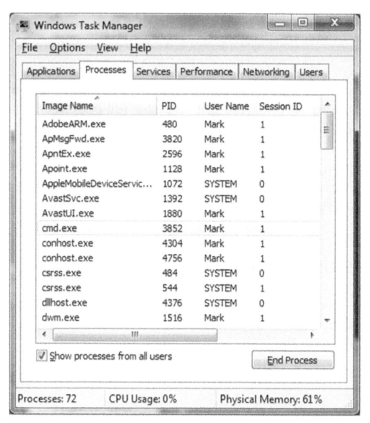

Figure 9.1: *Killing a Process using the Task Manager*

However, sometimes the process you need to kill is running under another user's credentials and Task Manager will not allow you to kill it. There is a solution. If you recall from the chapter on Batch Jobs, we learned that the *at* command submits jobs as the system user. Here we use that to our advantage.

To kill a job regardless of owner, we simply open a command prompt and submit a Task Manager process to start interactively within the next few minutes.

For example, if it is 9:58 AM when we need to do this, we tell it to start at 10:00 AM (2 minutes later).

```
C:\>  at 10:00 /interactive taskmgr.exe
```

When 10:00 AM arrives, a Task Manager window will pop up on your screen, running as System. From there you will have full permissions to kill any process you need to.

Now that we have seen how to kill processes using the Task Manager, we will move on to cover killing processes from the command prompt using the *taskkill* command.

Killing Processes Using *taskkill*

The way you delete processes from the command prompt is to use the *taskkill* command. The syntax is:

```
C:\>  taskkill /PID <process id>
```

So, for example, to delete process ID 223, you would type:

```
C:\>  taskkill /PID 223
```

The process ID can be found by executing the *tasklist* command, as seen in Figure 9.2.

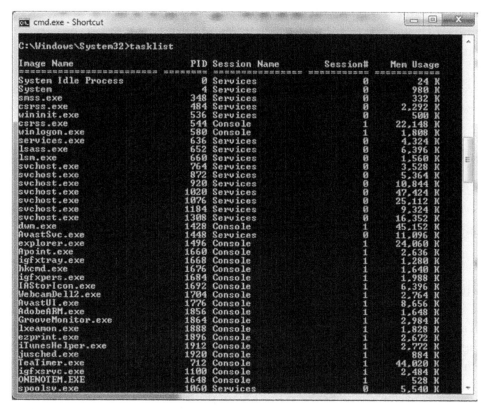

Figure 9.2: *Finding the Process ID*

A process can also be deleted by image name. For example, the iTunesHelper.exe could be deleted by the command:

```
C:\>  taskkill /IM iTunesHelper.exe
```

Or

```
C:\>  taskkill /PID 1912
```

There are also several switches that can be used. One of the more useful is the /F switch. It specifies to forcefully terminate the process, much like a *kill -9* does in UNIX/Linux.

For example, the following would forcefully delete our iTunesHelper.exe process.

```
C:\>  taskkill /PID 1912 /F
```

Now that we have seen how to use *taskkill* to end a process, let's move on to killing stuck services using the *sc queryex* command with *taskkill*.

Killing Stuck Services Using *sc queryex* and *taskkill*

Windows services can sometimes have a nasty habit of getting stuck in the stopping or starting state. Some believe that at this point there is no alternative but to reboot the server to clear the problem.

However, the following trick usually will work.

The first step is to right click and select *Properties* on the offending Windows service in order to find the actual service name. For example, when we look up the Distributed Transaction Coordinator service, we find that it is actually named MSDTC (Figure 9.3).

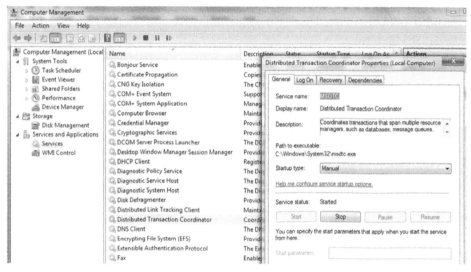

Figure 9.3: *Finding the Actual Service Name*

The next step is to do an *sc queryex* on the Windows service in order to find the Process ID, as seen in Figure 9.4

```
C:\Windows\System32>sc queryex "MSDTC"

SERVICE_NAME: MSDTC
        TYPE               : 10  WIN32_OWN_PROCESS
        STATE              : 4   RUNNING
                                 (STOPPABLE, NOT_PAUSABLE, ACCEPTS_SHUTDOWN)
        WIN32_EXIT_CODE    : 0   (0x0)
        SERVICE_EXIT_CODE  : 0   (0x0)
        CHECKPOINT         : 0x0
        WAIT_HINT          : 0x0
        PID                : 5180
        FLAGS              :

C:\Windows\System32>
```

Figure 9.4: *Using sc queryex to Find the Process ID*

The Process ID is 5180. So now we can issue the *taskkill /F* command on the process.

Another thing to remember: in Windows 2008, if we are not running the command prompt with *Run as administrator*, we will get an access denied error on the delete:

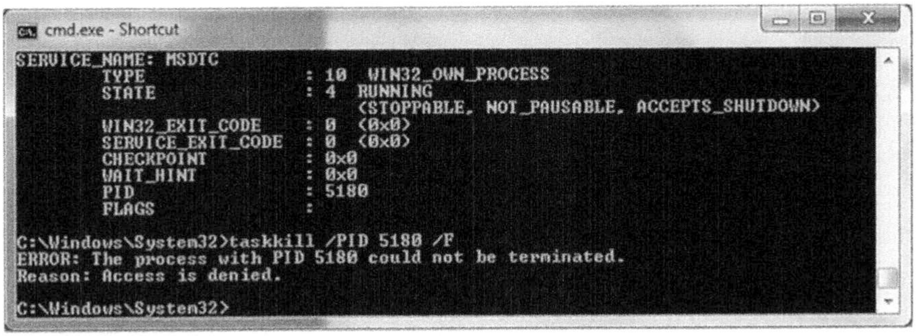

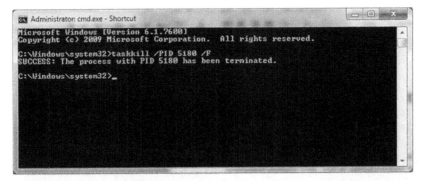

Figure 9.5: *Deleting a Process without Run as Administrator, Windows 2008*

Once we issue the same command in a command prompt window that we have opened with *Run as administrator*, we can successfully complete the delete:

Figure 9.6: *Deleting a Process with Run as Administrator, Windows 2008*

Summary

There are several ways to delete processes in Windows. This chapter has demonstrated three of the most useful ways, including the Task Manager, *taskkill* command, and *sc queryex* with the *taskkill* command. As in any other Operating System, please be very careful before doing so... you could very well crash your server!

The main points of this chapter include:

- There are several types of "rogue" processes that require killing inside Windows.

- You can query v$session to find processes that exist in Windows but do not exist in Oracle.

- You can use the online task manager to kill any process

- You can also use the *taskkill* and *sc* commands to nuke an Oracle process on Windows.

The next chapter will move on to examine how to manage Oracle installs and upgrades on Windows.

Windows Installs and Upgrades

10

Introduction

Unlike UNIX/Linux, Windows Servers are far more susceptible to internet viruses, and this is only one reason why it is a best practice to update your Windows operating system.

Remember, you DON'T have to apply patches, and sometimes patches can CAUSE unplanned issues. The best practices are always to conduct a full stress test in a TEST environment before applying the patches in production. It also depends on your production policy. In many shops, patches are only applied to address a specific known problem.

In general, there are two approaches to applying Oracle patches:

1. **If it ain't broke - don't fix it:** Don't apply Oracle patches and risk hitting new bugs.

2. **Apply all patches and be proactive:** Lots of extra work and you risk a patch causing a problem. This approach is especially recommended if the Windows Server has Internet access.

There are several things to look for when installing and patching Oracle on Windows. Here are some important things to keep in mind during Oracle installs and upgrades:

- **Stop Services:** Oracle services should be stopped first, before any upgrade or patch. The Distributed Transaction Process service should be stopped before any upgrade or patch. With 11gR2, sometimes the Windows Management Instrumentation service will have DLLs open.

- **Remove Antivirus software**: Antivirus should be stopped before any upgrade or patch. It is not a good idea to expose your Windows Server to the Internet, and antivirus software can kill performance.

- **Stop Backup Agents**: Backup agents (Backup Exec, DataProtector, etc.) should be stopped before any upgrade or patch.

- **Find and close open DLL's**: *tasklist /m filename.dll* should be used to find process IDs for open DLLs. If the Installer or OPatch still complains about an open DLL, even after you have killed the related process, try logging off and logging back on. If all else fails when the Installer complains about an open DLL, set the Oracle services to Manual and reboot the server!

- **Unset ORACLE_HOME parameter**: The ORACLE_HOME environment variable setting can cause TNS Protocol Adapter errors and more. Oracle says not to set this at all.

- **Adjust PATH variable**: The last product you install will be first in the PATH.

- **Re-start listener service**: After an install or upgrade, you must manually start listener with *LSNRCTL* to create the new listener service.

This chapter will review each of the above items in more detail. Let's begin with the importance of stopping all Oracle-related services before an Oracle install or upgrade.

Stopping Oracle Related Services

Prior to an upgrade or OPatch, the OracleServiceSID, Oracle listener, and other Oracle services need to be stopped. If these services are not stopped, there will be open DLLs that cannot be replaced by the Installer. An example is shown in the following two figures.

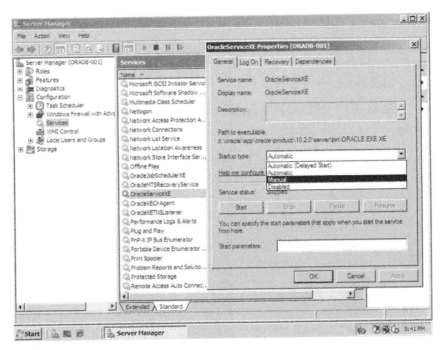

Figure 10.1: *Stopping Oracle-related Services*

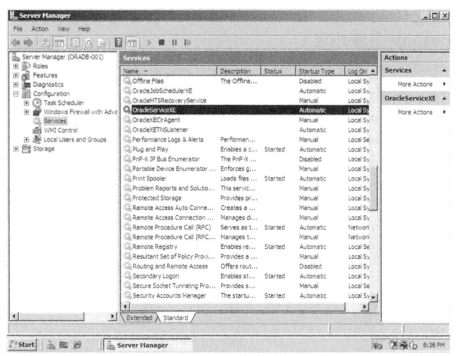

Figure 10.2: *Stopping Oracle-related Services*

In addition to stopping Oracles services, it's important to stop the Distributed Transaction Coordinator service, as described in the next section.

Stopping the Windows Distributed Transaction Coordinator Service

Prior to an upgrade or OPatch, we must also be sure to stop the Windows Distributed Transaction Coordinator. This Windows service coordinates transactions that span multiple resource managers, such as databases, message queues, and file systems, and as such may have Oracle files/DLLs open.

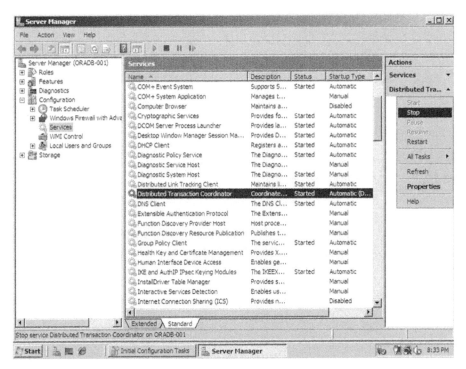

Figure 10.3: *Stopping the Distributed Transaction Coordinator*

If you are using Oracle 11gR2, the Windows Management Instrumentation service will also need to be stopped. This item will be covered next.

Stopping the Windows Management Instrumentation Service (Oracle 11gR2)

On Oracle 11gR2 on a Windows 64bit Operating System, the OPatch utility may show DLLs open, and a *tasklist /m* will show they are opened by a process called *wmiprvse.exe*. That would be the Windows Management Instrumentation service. When you stop the service, it may also inform you that some others, such as IP Helper, will also be stopped. Make a note of those.

Once these are stopped, the DLLs should be released. Please remember to start them all again when patching is complete.

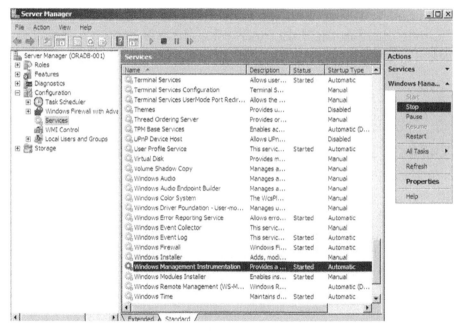

Figure 10.4: *Stopping Windows Management Instrumentation*

The next thing to consider is stopping antivirus or backup software.

Stopping Antivirus or Backup Software

Prior to an upgrade or OPatch, we must also be sure to stop any antivirus or backup software or agents running on the server. This is to both improve performance of the install/upgrade as well as to keep the antivirus or backup software from locking up any Oracle related files or DLLs. Just please remember to start it back up again after you are done!

It is also important to find the owner of any open DLLs. This can be done as described in the next section.

Using *tasklist /m* to Find the Owner of Open DLLs

If the Oracle installer or OPatch reports a specific DLL being open, you can find out what has that DLL open using the *tasklist* utility. Recall the syntax is:

```
tasklist /m filename.dll
```

This returns all the processes that have that DLL open. You can then kill using the *taskkill* utility, as documented in Chapter 9.

Be careful when killing processes! It is best to see what the DDL is first, and confirm that it is not related to a Windows service that is currently running. If the name of the executable is unfamiliar, search the Internet to see if you can find out what it is.

A Note About the ORACLE_HOME Environment Variable

The ORACLE_HOME environment variable will not get reset by an upgrade. It will be left at the previous value or, more likely, it will be blank since some versions of the Oracle Installer clear it out by default.

This can cause TNS Protocol Adapter errors when trying to start the listener, ODBC datasources to fail, as well as other problems. It is a good practice to check this following any upgrades.

The Last Product Installed Will be the First in the PATH

The last Oracle Product installed will be the first thing in the PATH. This can get you in trouble!

For example, if you install the Oracle RDBMS Software and then the Oracle Agent, the Oracle Agent will be first in the PATH, and the first place Windows will look.

The same goes for when you install multiple versions of Oracle on the same server. You can change this with the Environment tab in Oracle Universal Installer.

PATH can be checked as seen in Figure 10.5. Go to *My Computer*, right click and select *Properties,* and then select *Advanced* to get to this screen.

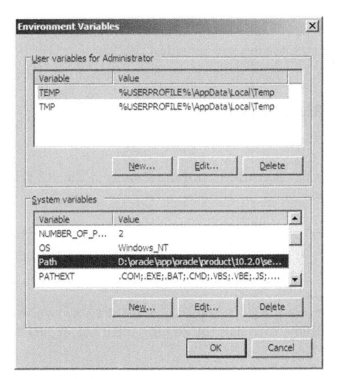

Figure 10.5: *Environment Variables, PATH*

A Note on Installing a New Listener

When you first install or upgrade to a new release of Oracle, you will notice there is no OracleListener Windows service. The first time you run LSNRCTL from the command prompt and issue a *start* command, provided you have a good listener.ora file, LSNRCTL will create the service for you.

There will be a *Failed to open service* error reported, but then it will go ahead and create the service. An example is next.

```
LSNRCTL> START
Starting tnslsnr: please wait...
```

```
Failed to open service <OracleOraHome11gTNSListener>, error 1060.
Service OracleOraHome11gTNSListener created, exe
<C:\Oracle\product\11.2.0.3\BIN\TNSLSNR >.
Service OracleOraHome11gTNSListener start pending.
Service OracleOraHome11gTNSListener started.
TNSLSNR for 64-bit Windows: Version 11.2.0.3.0 - Production
System parameter file is
C:\Oracle\product\11.2.0.3\network\admin\listener.ora
```

Remember, if you are a Windows 2008 user, you will need to start the command prompt by right clicking the *cmd.exe* icon and selecting *Run as administrator* for this to work properly.

Open DLLs – When All Else Fails...

If all else fails when the Installer complains about an open DLL, always try to logoff and log back on first. This sometimes clears things up and allows you to move on. If that does not work, the sure way to have all the Oracle DLLs closed is to set the Oracle services to Manual, as described in the Windows services chapter, and reboot the server! When it comes back up, none of the Oracle services will be started so the DLLs will all be closed and you can move forward with your install or patch. Remember to set everything back to Automatic when you are done!

Summary

This chapter discussed important things to consider prior to an Oracle install or upgrade on Windows. The surest way to avoid issues during Oracle installs, patches, and upgrades is to carefully read the release notes and installation guides, but the above tips can also be a great help.

The main points of this chapter include:

- Stopping certain services prior to an install or upgrade can prevent open DLLs.

- If DLLs are open, the *tasklist* utility can be used to find out what has it open.

- Be aware that the ORACLE_HOME environment variable will not get reset by an upgrade.

- Remember that the last Oracle product installed will be the first in the PATH.

Now that we understand how to manage Oracle installs and upgrades on Windows, the next chapter will examine how to manage Oracle on Windows using ORADIM.

Managing Oracle on Windows Using ORADIM

Introduction

Managing Oracle on Windows refers to controlling, stopping, starting, creating, and deleting Oracle services. As with most else in the Windows environment, there are several ways to manage Oracle services.

This chapter will review some of the most common commands to accomplish this, including ORADIM and the *net* command. The Services GUI can also be used, as described back in Chapter 6. The difference here is that ORADIM and *net* can be used at the command prompt, which also means they can be scripted as well.

We will also review why it is best to make arrangements (manually or via a script) to cleanly shut Oracle down before a server shutdown.

Let's begin with an overview of the ORADIM utility.

ORADIM

Oracle on Windows is delivered with a utility that is used exclusively for that Operating System – the ORADIM utility. Basically, ORADIM's mission in life is to create, delete, stop and start Oracle-related Windows services from the DOS command line.

In UNIX or Linux, when you create a database with a script, you use the *create database* command - that's all you need.

In Windows, you first need to create the Windows service. This is done with the ORADIM command. Again, ORADIM can also be used to stop, start, modify, and delete the service.

> **Note!** When using the Oracle Database Assistant or the *create database* option (when using the Oracle Universal Installer), creating the Windows service is done automatically for you.

To create the service, the general syntax is:

```
ORADIM -NEW -SID <sid> -INTPWD <password>
-MAXUSERS <number> -STARTMODE <auto, manual> -PFILE <full path to pfile>
```

Here is an actual example to create an instance named ORCL:

```
ORADIM -NEW -SID ORCL -INTPWD mypasswd -MAXUSERS 4 -STARTMODE auto -PFILE
C:\oracle\10g\database\initORCL.ora
```

This command performs the following tasks:

1. Creates the ORCL instance.
2. Creates the associated Windows service.
3. Sets the password to *mypasswd*.
4. Allows 4 users to connect as SYSDBA.
5. Sets the service to start automatically when Windows starts.
6. Uses a pfile named C:\oracle\10g\database\initORCL.ora.

A couple things to note here: first, the command must be entered entirely on one continuous line. Second, while this command creates the instance, it does NOT create the database. This you need to do using scripts or commands.

Again, if you use the Database Assistant or the Oracle Universal Installer, then the step of creating the Windows service is done for you.

ORADIM can also be used to delete a service. To delete the service, the general syntax is:

```
ORADIM -DELETE -SID <sid>
```

An example to delete the ORCL instance would be:

```
ORADIM -DELETE -SID ORCL
```

The database itself does NOT get deleted by this command, just the Windows service. Therefore, one could delete the service, recreate it using the same name, and restart the instance. All of the database files and contents would remain unchanged.

ORADIM can also be used to stop and start the Oracle Instance. The commands are as follows:

To shut down the service (and so the database/instance):

```
ORADIM -SHUTDOWN -SID <sid> -USRPWD / -SHUTTYPE SRVC -SHUTMODE <immediate,
normal, abort>
```

To shut down the database/instance but leave the service running:

```
ORADIM -SHUTDOWN -SID <sid> -USRPWD / -SHUTTYPE INST -SHUTMODE <immediate,
normal, abort>
```

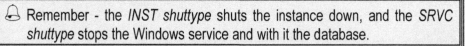 Remember - the *INST shuttype* shuts the instance down, and the *SRVC shuttype* stops the Windows service and with it the database.

As an example:

```
ORADIM -SHUTDOWN -SID ORCL -USRPWD / -SHUTTYPE SRVC -SHUTMODE i
```

One would generally want the shutdown to be immediate or abort; normal would hang until all users and transactions were completely done. That could take all day!

To startup:

```
ORADIM -STARTUP -SID <sid>
```

As an example:

```
ORADIM -STARTUP -SID ORCL
```

These stop and start commands can be quite handy to use when scripting shutdowns and startups, as well as for controlling things from the command line.

In addition to the Oracle Alert Log, there is an ORADIM.LOG in the ORACLE_HOME\database directory that tracks all instance shutdowns and startups, as seen in Figure 11.1. Looking in this file can confirm whenever your Oracle Instance has started or stopped.

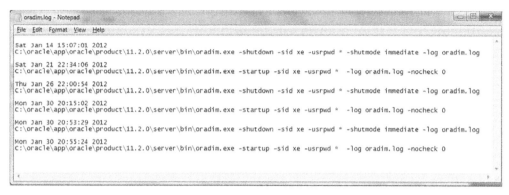

Figure 11.1: *ORADIM.LOG*

Now that we have reviewed the ORADIM utility, let's move on to briefly revisit the *net stop* and *net start* commands.

The *net stop* and *net start* Commands

In Chapter 6, we reviewed controlling Windows services using the *net stop* and *net start* commands.

These, as shown in Chapter 6, can be used to stop and start Oracle services from scripts and the command line.

Either ORADIM or *net* can be used effectively for those purposes.

How to Cleanly Shut Down Your Oracle Database When Windows is Shut Down

If you recall, we reviewed Oracle services in Chapter 6 and discussed the Registry Settings controlling the Oracle services in Chapter 4.

The Registry Setting *ORA_SID_SHUTDOWN*, when set to *TRUE*, is supposed to tell Windows to cleanly shut down the instance when the service is stopped. This is done as advertised as long as the server is running, but it does not work if the Windows Server crashes quickly.

So, for example, we can issue a *net stop* command, an *ORADIM SHUTDOWN*, or use the Windows GUI to stop an Oracle Instance while the server is running. In this case, we get a shutdown done however we tell it (immediate, abort, normal), as we expect. This is because the server is still up and running, and Windows is able to complete the Oracle shutdown.

However, when the server (and so the Operating System itself) is being shut down, Windows stops the Oracle service which in turn tries try to stop the instance, but it never gets to completely shut Oracle down. Specifically, once the Windows shutdown has commenced, the *security.dll* is unregistered before the Oracle shutdown command has time to execute properly.

The end result is that the Operating System literally gets taken out from under the running Oracle Instance, without it having the chance to execute any sort of clean shutdown. This is, needless to say, a less than ideal situation!

Oracle documents this clearly in Metalink Note 231495.1 – *ORA_SID_SHUTDOWN Registry Parameter not working as Documented.*

To be sure your database gets cleanly shut down whenever the server is shut down, it is important to either manually stop the Oracle services before every server shutdown, or to write a script that runs upon server shutdown. The other option is to set SQLNET.AUTHENTICATION_SERVICES to *NONE* in your SQLNET.ORA file. This, however, will have the result of not allowing you to connect as sysdba.

It is quite painless to create an Oracle Shutdown script, place it in the proper Windows Directory, and then tell Windows to execute it whenever a server shutdown occurs. This is done as follows. First,

---

create a simple shutdown script using notepad.exe. An example is below. (The :: denotes a comment line, and we will name our script StopOracleServices.bat)

```
::
:: StopOracleServices.bat
::
:: This script is used to gracefully stop ORCL Services
::
::

net stop OracleServiceORCL

::
::   done
::

    EXIT
```

Second, we will copy this script to the directory:

```
C:\Windows\System\GroupPolicy\Machine\Scripts\Shutdown
```

Third, we will tell Windows that it needs to be run whenever the server is shut down, using the Group Policy Editor. To run the Group Policy Editor, go to *Start, Run,* and then type *gpedit.msc* and click *OK,* as shown in Figure 11.2.

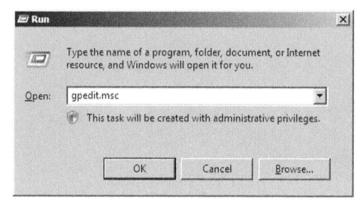

Figure 11.2: *Running the Group Policy Editor*

This will bring up the Local Group Policy Editor.

On the left pane go to *Computer Configuration*, *Windows Settings*, click *Scripts (Startup/Shutdown)*, and click *Shutdown* in the right pane.

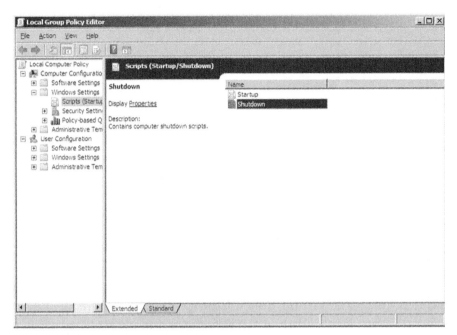

Figure 11.3: *Local Group Policy Editor*

Clicking *Shutdown* will display the *Shutdown Properties* screen. Here click *Add* (Figure 11.4).

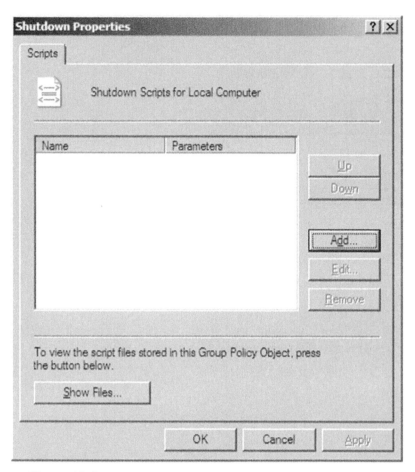

Figure 11.4: *Shutdown Properties*

Once you have clicked *Add*, you will be prompted to select the file to run at shutdown. Here, click the *Browse* button as shown in Figure 11.5.

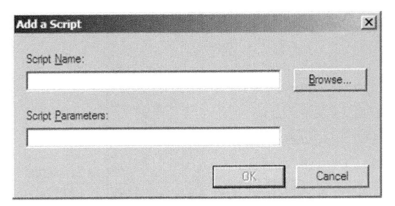

Figure 11.5: *Selecting the File to Run at Shutdown*

Once *Browse* is clicked, you will be able to navigate to the file we copied to

```
C:\Windows\System32\GroupPolicy\Machine\Scripts\Shutdown.
```

Next, select the *StopOracleServices.bat* file and click *Open*, as seen in Figure 11.6.

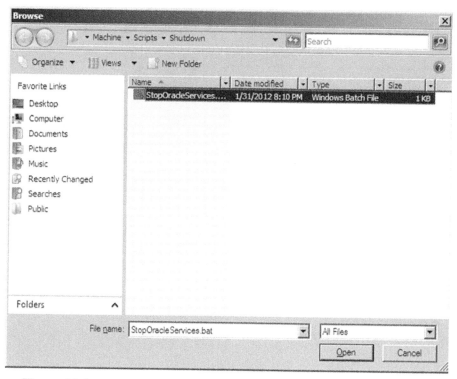

Figure 11.6: *Selecting the File to Run at Shutdown*

Once you have clicked *Open*, a popup window with the script name will appear (Figure 11.7). Here, click *OK*.

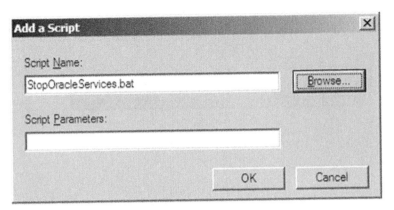

Figure 11.7: *Adding a Script*

This will bring you back to the *Shutdown Properties* screen. Click *OK* to complete (Figure 11.8).

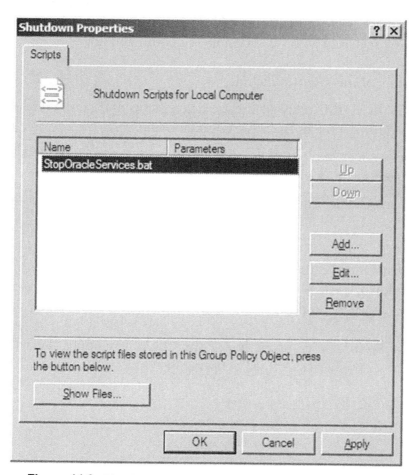

Figure 11.8: *Shutdown Properties*

Now whenever Windows is shut down, the script will be run and Oracle will be safely shut down before the server is shut down.

Summary

ORADIM is a Windows-only utility for creating, deleting, stopping, and starting Oracle services in the Windows environment. It can be quite useful for many scenarios in both scripting and command line.

The main points of this chapter include:

- Using the ORADIM utility to create, delete, stop and start Oracle-related Windows services from the command line.

- Using the *net start* and *net stop* commands to stop and start Oracle services from scripts and the command line.

- Creating an Oracle Shutdown script to cleanly shut down your database.

Remember that Oracle cannot control Windows past a certain point on a server shutdown, so it is critical to be sure you shut your databases down prior to a server shutdown.

Now we have seen how to properly use the ORADIM utility, we will move on to cover the basics of Shell Scripting in Windows.

Shell Scripting Basics

Introduction

Shell scripting refers to organizing native Windows commands into scripts using the simple notepad editor. These commands can be arranged into programs, or scripts, that can help with many Oracle DBA tasks.

This chapter will not be covering Windows Powershell or any other more complex means of creating scripts, but will instead demonstrate how piecing Windows commands together can make our jobs easier.

The technique and the coding style used in the scripts in the next chapter reflect the author's many years as a Basic Plus programmer (which may explain the use of *gotos* and drop through logic). There are many other ways to piece the commands together, so feel free to take what you learn from these examples and use it how you wish. Whatever works best for you!

Let's Get Started

There are commands that can rename files, list directories, submit batch jobs, search files for specific items, take actions based on the results, and many other things. The next sections will review some of the most useful commands and their syntax. We will then put them together into simple but useful scripts in the next chapter.

Please remember that any Windows command can be used in these scripts, limited only by your imagination and ingenuity.

Let's begin by covering why it is important to comment on your code.

Commenting on Code

Commenting your code is critical. It allows others who are reading your scripts to understand what each section is doing, including you if you happen to be looking at it sometime after it was developed!

There are two ways to indicate comments: REM and ::

For example,

```
REM
REM    This script clears out excess archivelogs
REM
```

is equivalent to

```
::
::    This script clears out excess archivelogs
::
```

Next, let's look at the *goto* command.

The *goto* Command

The *goto* command will send your script to whatever section you tell it, usually used after some condition is met. The destination is a section of code with a name, preceded by a colon.

For example, the command

```
goto exit_now
```

will jump to the code section that has the tag

```
:exit_now
```

Redirecting Output to a File

Outputting the results of a command to a file is a very basic but important task. It allows you to do such things as run a command, save the results to a file, and search it later on in the script.

The syntax is simply:

```
command > full path to output file
```

For example, the command

```
net start > c:\adminscripts\output\services.txt
```

will list the running Windows services to a file called services.txt in the folder c:\adminscripts\output.

The following commands, *find* and *findstr*, can be used against such output files.

The *findstr* and *find* Commands

As discussed in Chapter 1, there are two different commands to search for text. *Find* is very basic and searches for a single string in a file and returns the resultant line. The other, *findstr*, is far more powerful. *Findstr* searches for a single string, multiple strings, or an exact phrase.

For example:

- *find abc* finds the string "abc"

- *findstr "abc"* finds the string "abc"

- *findstr "abc 123"* finds strings "abc" or "123"

- *findstr /C:"abc 123"* finds the exact phrase "abc 123"

These can be used to search for single or multiple strings or phrases in logfiles. This is perfect for searching the Oracle Alert Log for ORA-errors.

Now let's see how to use the *forfiles* command.

The *forfiles* Command

The *forfiles* command searches for a given set of files and then performs a specified action on the returned set of files.

For example, the command below finds all files in the D:\oracle\archives folder that are older than 7 days, and does a directory of those files.

```
forfiles -p D:\oracle\archives -m *.* -d -7 -c "cmd /c dir @FILE"
```

The command below is similar. It finds all files in the D:\oracle\archives folder that are older than 7 days, and then performs a delete on the result set.

```
forfiles -p D:\oracle\archives -m *.* -d -7 -c "cmd /c del/q @FILE"
```

The switches used above are:

-p = the folder to perform the action against.
-m = the filenames (*.* or *.ext or any other legal filename).

-d = the number of days. -7 was seven days before today.

-c = execute the command against the result set.

cmd /c = the Windows command to start a new command shell, execute the following and then terminate.

@FILE = the result set from the *forfiles* command to execute against.

Next is a brief overview of renaming and datastamping files.

How to Rename or Datestamp Files

Renaming or datestamping files are important in scripting. This is especially true for automating things such as Oracle Exports, where you may want to keep several revisions of output and not write over them each time. Two simple ways to do this follow.

Method one is to rotate filenames using a number or whatever other scheme you choose, using the rename and delete commands. The routine below deletes the oldest file, and then renames the rest up one number. Each time this is executed, the oldest file is deleted and the export files are renamed so that five revisions are saved and the output file used for *expdp* will not exist, avoiding an *output file already exists* error. One of the beauties of this method is that you never need to run a cleanup script, since there will always be a fixed number of output files.

```
del d:\oracle\oradata\orcl\exp\orcl_export5.*
ren d:\oracle\oradata\orcl\exp\orcl_export4.* orcl_export5.*
ren d:\oracle\oradata\orcl\exp\orcl_export3.* orcl_export4.*
ren d:\oracle\oradata\orcl\exp\orcl_export2.* orcl_export3.*
ren d:\oracle\oradata\orcl\exp\orcl_export1.* orcl_export2.*
ren d:\oracle\oradata\orcl\exp\orcl_export.* orcl_export1.*
```

Method two uses the *date* command. The routine below sets a variable called *datestamp* to portions of today's date, and uses the *ren* command to concatenate that as a file extension to your file. Using this method will necessitate deleting extra files so that you do not accumulate too many.

The date is returned as a DDD MM/DD/YYYY string:

```
C:\>echo %DATE%
Mon 09/10/2012
```

The command below parses the output of *date* and takes the 10th character for 4 positions, the 4th for 2, and the 7th for 2 and builds a YYYYMMDD extension to add to the filename. The starting position is always zero, not 1.

```
set DATESTAMP=%DATE:~10,4%%DATE:~4,2%%DATE:~7,2%
ren c:\adminscripts\logs\export.log export.%DATESTAMP%
C:\>echo %DATESTAMP%
20120910
```

So, the resultant filename would be:

```
C:\adminscripts\logs\export.20120910
```

Now that we've covered datestamping, let's look at how to pause in a script using *sleep.exe* or *ping*.

How to Sleep

Sometimes it is necessary to pause in a script, such as when shutting down the Oracle service prior to a cold backup to be sure it is completely shut down before continuing.

Sleep.exe, found in the Windows 2000 Resource Kit, can be used for this purpose. This executable allows a batch file to sleep for *n* seconds.

The *ping* command may also be used. The syntax is:

```
ping -n seconds+1 127.0.0.1>nul
```

For example, the following would be used to sleep for 20 seconds:

```
C:\> ping -n 20 127.0.0.1>nul
```

Now let's take a look at the *blat* and *soon.exe* utilities.

Two Handy Utilities

Blat.exe is a public domain program to send emails. What *blat* does is forward the email to your email spooler/server.

Blat is very simple to use; just download the utility, place *blat.exe* in the c:\windows\system32 folder, and point it to your email server. Once you've done that, you can use the *blat* command to send emails from scripts. The *blat* website is www.blat.net.

The syntax for the initial setup (only done once) is the *blat* command, followed by the install switch, the SMTP spooler name (your email server name typically), and the userid you want the email to appear as the sender:

```
Blat -install <SMTP_spoolername> <useridyouwantemailfrom>
```

Example:

```
C$> Blat -install  my_smtp.edu  OracleEmail
```

The syntax for using *blat* to send an email is:

```
Blat <filename> -t <destination emailaddress> -s <subject>
```

Example:

```
C:> blat D:\export\exp.log -t dba@email.com -s "Exp complete"
```

Soon.exe, found in the Windows 2000 Resource Kit, allows you to run a batch job every *xx* seconds.

Here is an example of rerunning a script every 2 minutes using *soon.exe*:

```
c:\soon\soon.exe 0120 c:\adminscripts\uptime\check_DBSvc.cmd
```

Putting it all together

Now that we have some basic commands, we can put them all together. In Windows, any file with a .bat extension is considered an executable batch file. This is the type of file we will place our commands in. The .cmd extension can also be used, which is a legacy from 16bit Windows that still works, with some reported exceptions in Windows XP.

The best way to demonstrate is to give examples, so the next chapter will present some simple scripts that perform common Oracle DBA tasks.

Summary

Windows commands can be used to program simple and even complex scripts, and can be created using the notepad utility. These scripts can be executed online or submitted as scheduled tasks, which is where their real power lies.

The main points of this chapter include:

- Commenting on code
- Using the *goto* command
- Redirecting output to a file

- Using the *find* and *findstr* commands

- Renaming or datestamping files

- Pausing a script using *sleep.exe* or *ping*

- Using *blat* and *soon.exe*

Now let's delve deeper into the subject by looking at some working examples of Windows shell scripts in the next chapter.

Windows Shell Scripts

Introduction

As stated earlier, any file with a .bat extension is considered an executable batch file, which is the type of file the commands will be placed in. The .cmd extension can also be used, which is a legacy from 16bit Windows that still works, with some reported exceptions in Windows XP.

However, writing Oracle scripts in a Windows environment can be problematic, but there are some important secrets for deploying Oracle scripts in a Windows Server.

Oracle-only Scripts in Windows

The only time it's necessary to have a script reside in a Windows environment is when something needs to be done to the Windows files. Even in these cases, PL/SQL can be written to use the *utl_file* utility to read flat files on Windows.

For Oracle-only tasks in Windows, it's best to write scripts using the *dbms_job* or *dbms_scheduler* packages.

Types of Oracle Scripts in Windows

There are several choices for writing Oracle scripts in a Windows environment:

- **DOS bat files**: Microsoft enhanced the DOS command functions starting with Windows 2000. However, DOS commands were still nowhere near as powerful as a UNIX shell script.

- **MKS Toolkit**: A way to run UNIX shell scripts in Windows

- **Cygwin**: The CYGWIN product that supports UNIX shell scripting

- **SFU**: Microsoft released Windows Services For UNIX (SFU) to more closely emulate a variety of UNIX shells and UNIX utilities to ease the migration from a UNIX to a Windows environment. While SFU is certainly a more comprehensive solution than the native command prompt, it is more complicated and does not provide total compatibility for porting UNIX scripts to Windows.

- **UnixDos**: The UnixDosToolkit from Professional Software Solutions provides all of the UNIX-like functions.

- **Windows PowerShell for Oracle**: This is a new command line interface for Windows.

The next section will review some simple Oracle commands within an executable *bat* file using Windows DOS commands.

Sample Invocation of Oracle from Windows

The DOS command line can interface to Oracle, and we see this working Windows *bat* file executable with an embedded SQL*Plus call. The trick is that the SQL*Plus invocation spool the output on a single command line:

```
sqlplusw -s "%DBUser%/%DBPass%@%DBTNS%" @%LOG%OraCall.sql   >
%LOG%OraCall.lst
```

Here is a Windows Oracle script with DOS commands to set the environment:

```
@ECHO off
SET DBUser=%1
SET DBPass=%2
SET DBTNS=%3
SET LOG=\temp\test\

ECHO spool %LOG%OraCall.log                                          >
%LOG%OraCall.sql
ECHO set linesize 132                                               >>
%LOG%OraCall.sql
ECHO COL x_tns      NEW_VALUE v_tns      NOPRINT                    >>
%LOG%OraCall.sql
ECHO COL x_dbid     NEW_VALUE v_dbid     NOPRINT                    >>
%LOG%OraCall.sql
ECHO COL x_dbname   NEW_VALUE v_dbname   NOPRINT                    >>
%LOG%OraCall.sql
ECHO SELECT '%DBTNS%'  x_tns      FROM dual;                        >>
%LOG%OraCall.sql
ECHO SELECT dbid      x_dbid     FROM v$database;                   >>
%LOG%OraCall.sql
ECHO SELECT name      x_dbname   FROM v$database;                   >>
%LOG%OraCall.sql
ECHO @SQLSelect.sql                                                >>
%LOG%OraCall.sql
ECHO spool off                                                     >>
%LOG%OraCall.sql
ECHO exit                                                          >>
%LOG%OraCall.sql
sqlplusw -s "%DBUser%/%DBPass%@%DBTNS%" @%LOG%OraCall.sql   >
%LOG%OraCall.lst
```

The following are examples of shell scripts to perform various DBA tasks that are critical to all administration in Windows.

Obviously, these are only example scripts, so you will need to substitute your service names, Oracle SID names, folder structures, etc. in order for these to become working scripts in your environment.

Remember that the double-colon string :: in Windows Scripting denotes a comment. Commenting your code is always a good practice, especially when working with complex Oracle Windows scripts.

Another good practice with scripts is to create a folder on the Oracle Server at the location:

```
C:\Adminscripts
```

Then, separate subfolders are created for each type of script. For example:

```
C:\Adminscripts\backups - backup scripts
C:\Adminscripts\exports - export scripts
```

The above directory would keep export and import scripts.

Oracle Shutdown Script for Windows

A normal shutdown of an Oracle database is actually rarely used. This is because the normal shutdown waits for everyone to complete their work and then logoff in an orderly fashion. When a normal shutdown occurs, the database is closed in a normal manner, and all changes made in the database are flushed to the database datafiles. This is known as a "clean shutdown."

Most of the time this is not practical. There always seems to be someone who has left and forgot to log out, or there are times that Oracle processes become "zombied" (this is where Oracle thinks someone is connected to the database but they really are not). In these cases, the database will never come down; it will simply wait forever until you manually kill those sessions. Because of this, we often recommend the *shutdown immediate* or *shutdown abort* commands, which we will discuss in the next sections. Here is an example of the use of the normal shutdown command:

```
SQL> shutdown
```

When you execute a shutdown, Oracle will flush all the changes in memory out to the database datafiles. This makes database startup quicker because the database is in a consistent state.

Think of it this way: if you jump into the air and land on your feet, you have landed in a way that prepares you to make another jump. If you jump and land on your back, you are in no position to make another jump; instead, you must perform a recovery by taking the actions required to stand again. A clean shutdown is one that is prepared to come back up without delay. A dirty shutdown is one that lands on its back; it cannot come back up without first recovering itself.

Shutdown Immediate

Perhaps the best way to initially shutdown the database is the *shutdown immediate* command. This command will prevent any new logins, then rollback any uncommitted transactions, and then bring down the database.

In the process of bringing down the database, Oracle will flush all the changes in memory out to the database datafiles too, just like a regular shutdown does. This makes database startup quicker. Here is an example of shutting down a database with the *shutdown immediate* command:

```
SQL> shutdown immediate
```

The *shutdown immediate* command will work most of the time, but there are times when it can hang and fail to shut down the database. In these cases, the *shutdown abort* command is called for.

Shutdown Abort

The *shutdown abort* command is pretty much a guaranteed way to get the database to shut down.

It is a "hard crash" of the database, and this can result in a longer time to start the database back up. Still, it can't really hurt the database using the *shutdown abort* command, and there may be more than a few occasions where it is necessary to use the *shutdown abort* command.

At times, the *shutdown abort* can be the shutdown method of choice, since there may be times when it is necessary to force the database down. Here is an example using the *shutdown abort* command:

```
SQL> shutdown  abort
```

If it's necessary to perform a specialized Oracle shutdown, such as a *shutdown abort,* a SQL*Plus script can be used. In Windows, SQL*Plus can be invoked in a *bat* file. The trick is to put the whole SQL*Plus command on a single line:

```
c:> type run_oracle.bat

@echo OFF
set MYDIR=C:\oracle\scripts
SQL*Plus -s fred/flintstone @%MYDIR%\shutdown_oracle.sql
exit
```

The following is an example of a generic script to shut down Oracle on Windows. This is a very basic Oracle Windows script, because it simply stops the Oracle service and the listener. The *net stop* command is used but ORADIM can also be used; however, *net stop* avoids issues with PATH and ORACLE_HOME and so is safer to use.

🖫 shutdown_oracle_windows.bat

```
::
:: StopOracleServices.bat
::
:: This script is used to gracefully stop ORCL Instance and Services
::
:: show running services before shutdown
net start > c:\adminscripts\logs\preshutdown.log

::
::   stop the Listener
::
net stop OracleListener10g
::
:: Graceful DB shutdown
::
net stop OracleServiceORCL

:: show running services after shutdown
net start > c:\adminscripts\logs\postshutdown.log

::
::   done
::
Exit
```

At shutdown time, it is not always necessary to stop the listener, but it is in the script to show that it is possible. This script also does a *net start* and places the output to log files before and after to show that the services were indeed shutdown successfully.

Next, let's look at a startup script for Oracle on Windows.

Oracle Startup Script for Windows

The Oracle database is started with the *startup* command. In order to do this, the user must first be logged into an account that has sysdba or sysoper privileges such as the SYS account. Here is an example of a DBA connecting to a database and starting the instance in Windows:

```
C:\Documents and Settings\Mark>set oracle_sid=booktst

C:\Documents and Settings\Mark>SQL*Plus "sys as sysdba"

SQL*Plus: Release 10.1.0.2.0 - Production on Mon Feb 21 12:35:48
```

```
Enter password: xxxx
Connected to an idle instance.

SQL> startup
ORACLE instance started.

Total System Global Area   251658240 bytes
Fixed Size                    788368 bytes
Variable Size              145750128 bytes
Database Buffers           104857600 bytes
Redo Buffers                  262144 bytes
Database mounted.
Database opened.
```

In this example from a Windows XP server, we set the ORACLE_SID to the name of the database and we log into SQL*Plus using the "sys as sysdba" login. This gives us the privileges we need to be able to startup the database. Finally, after we enter our password, we issue the startup command to startup the database. Oracle displays its progress as it opens the database, and then returns us to the SQL*Plus prompt once the startup has been completed.

When Oracle is trying to open your database, it goes through three distinct stages, and each of these is listed in the startup output listed previously. These stages are:

- Startup (nomount)

- Mount

- Open

Let's look at these stages in a bit more detail.

The Startup (nomount) Stage

When the startup command is issued, the first thing the database will do is enter the nomount stage. During the nomount stage, Oracle first opens and reads the initialization parameter file (init.ora) to see how the database is configured. For example, the sizes of all of the memory areas in Oracle are defined within the parameter file.

After the parameter file is accessed, the memory areas associated with the database instance are allocated. Also, during the nomount stage, the Oracle background processes are started. Together, we call these processes and the associated allocated memory the Oracle instance.

Once the instance has started successfully, the database is considered to be in the nomount stage. If you issue the startup command, then Oracle will automatically move onto the next stage of the startup, the mount stage.

Starting the Oracle Instance (Nomount Stage)

There are some types of Oracle recovery operations that require the database to be in nomount stage. When this is the case, a special startup command needs to be issued: *startup nomount*, as seen in this example:

```
SQL> startup nomount
```

The Mount Stage

When the startup command enters the mount stage, it opens and reads the control file. The control file is a binary file that tracks important database information, such as the location of the database datafiles.

In the mount stage, Oracle determines the location of the datafiles, but does not yet open them. Once the datafile locations have been identified, the database is ready to be opened.

Mounting the Database

Some forms of recovery require that the database be opened in mount stage. To put the database in mount stage, use the *startup mount* command as seen here:

```
SQL> startup mount
```

If you have already started the database instance with the *startup nomount* command, you might change it from the nomount to mount startup stage using the *alter database* command:

```
SQL> alter database mount;
```

The Open Oracle Startup Stage

The last startup step for an Oracle database is the open stage. When Oracle opens the database, it accesses all of the datafiles associated with the database. Once it has accessed the database datafiles, Oracle makes sure that all of the database datafiles are consistent.

Opening the Oracle Database

To open the database, you can just use the *startup* command as seen in this example:

```
SQL> startup
```

If the database is mounted, you can open it with the *alter database open* command as seen in this example:

```
SQL> alter database open;
```

Opening the Database in Restricted Mode

You can also start the database in restricted mode. Restricted mode will only allow users with special privileges to access the database (typically DBAs), even though the database is technically open. We use the *startup restrict* command to open the database in restricted mode as seen in this example:

```
SQL> startup restrict
```

You can take the database in and out of restricted mode with the *alter database* command, as seen in this example:

```
-- Put the database in restricted session mode.

SQL> alter system enable restricted session;

-- Take the database out of restricted session mode.

SQL> alter system disable restricted session;
```

> 🔔 **Note:** Any users connected to the Oracle instance when going into restricted mode will remain connected; they must be manually disconnected from the database by exiting gracefully or by the DBA with the *alter system kill session* command.

This next script simply starts the Oracle service and the listener. It also rotates the SQL*Net listener logs, assuming the listener was shut down when Oracle was shut down.

This is a good way to automate SQL*Net log rotation but is not always necessary. A separate script could be created that stops the listener, rotates the logs, and restarts it. That script is next.

💾 startup_oracle_windows.bat

```
::
:: StartOracleServices.bat
::
```

```
:: This script is used to start the ORCL service
::
::   rotate logs
::
set DATESTAMP=%DATE:~10,4%%DATE:~4,2%%DATE:~7,2%
ren c:\oracle\10.2.0\network\log\listener.log listener.%DATESTAMP%
ren c:\oracle\10.2.0\network\log\SQL*Net.log SQL*Net.%DATESTAMP%
::
::   start DB and Listener
::
net start OracleServiceORCL
net start OracleListener10g
::
::   All Done
::
Exit
```

Now let's look at a script to rotate our SQL*Net logs.

Rotate SQL*Net Logs – Stopping the Listener

This script simply stops the listener, rotates the logs, and restarts it. This is a good way to automate SQL*Net log rotation separately from database shutdowns and restarts. Note that the listener will be down for the amount of time this is running!

🖫 rotate_sql_net_logs_oracle_windows.bat

```
::
:: RotateListenerLogs
::
:: This script is used to rotate the Oracle  Listener Logs
::
net stop OracleListener10g
::
::   rotate logs
::
set DATESTAMP=%DATE:~10,4%%DATE:~4,2%%DATE:~7,2%
ren c:\oracle\10.2.0\network\log\listener.log listener.%DATESTAMP%
ren c:\oracle\10.2.0\network\log\SQL*Net.log SQL*Net.%DATESTAMP%
::
::   start Listener
::
net start OracleListener10g
::
::   All Done
::
Exit
```

Rotate SQL*Net Logs – Not Stopping the Listener

Starting in 11gR2, the listener log is not activated by default. You have to turn on listener logging:

```
logging_listener_name=on
```

The great thing about this is that all the OS logs and database logs can now be viewed in the same remote log using a SQL query, as will be shown.

First, create a directory to query the listener logs via SQL.

To create a directory object to be queried using SQL:

💾 query_listener_log_SQL.sql

```
create directory LISTENERDIR
as '/u01/app/oracle/oracle/product/10.2.0/db_4/network/log'
/

create table listenerlog
(
   logtime1 timestamp,
   connect1 varchar2(300),
   protocol1 varchar2(300),
   action1 varchar2(15),
   service1 varchar2(15),
   return1 number(10)
)
organization external (
   type oracle_loader
   default directory LISTENERDIR
   access parameters
   (
      records delimited by newline
      nobadfile
      nologfile
      nodiscardfile
      fields terminated by "*" lrtrim
      missing field values are null
      (
         logtime1 char(30) date_format
         date mask "DD-MON-YYYY HH24:MI:SS",
         connect1,
         protocol1,
```

```
        action1,
        service1,
        return1
    )
  )
  location ('listener.log')
)
reject limit unlimited
/
```

The above script allows us to have an external table that makes the listener log appear as if it was rows in a relational table, and the rows can be queried via native SQL instead of Windows utilities.

This next script rotates the SQL*Net logs without stopping the listener. It sets *log_status* off, renames the logfile, and sets log status back on.

🖫 **rotate_logs_listener_oracle_windows.bat**

```
::
:: RotateListenerLogs2
::
:: This script is used to rotate the Oracle  Listener Logs without stopping
::
Lsnrctl set log_status off
::
::   rotate logs
::
set DATESTAMP=%DATE:~10,4%%DATE:~4,2%%DATE:~7,2%
ren c:\oracle\10.2.0\network\log\listener.log listener.%DATESTAMP%
ren c:\oracle\10.2.0\network\log\SQL*Net.log SQL*Net.%DATESTAMP%
::
::   start logging again
::
lsnrctl set log_status on
::
::   All Done
::
Exit
```

Next, let's look at a script to do data pump exports and imports.

Data Pump Export

Oracle Data pump provides an integrated tool to move the data among the database systems. Data pump is a high speed, parallel infrastructure that enables data and metadata to be quickly moved to another database. Data pump export and data pump imports are the enhanced versions of the original export and import tools.

The executable program for Oracle Data Pump export is named *expdp*, and is located in the $ORACLE_HOME/bin directory. The *expdp* executable can read a list of directives, as specified by the *parfile* option to *expdp*.

Below is an example of an export parameter file: *export_options.par*.

```
compress=n
direct=n
buffer=1000
tables=table_with_one_million_rows
userid=scott/tiger
```

Using this parameter file, the export command line is executed by the following:

```
expdp parfile=export_options.par
```

You can add a *where* clause to your export syntax to extract a sub-set of your production rows. In this example, we restrict the export to rows added in the last month:

```
expdp scott/tiger tables=tab1, tab2 query="where mymonth > sysdate - 31"
```

You can generate syntax for all tables in your schema by building the export syntax with a query against *user_tables*.

All About expdp

Data Pump Export (*expdp*) is a very modern, server based and highly scalable data unloading utility. On typical multi-processor servers with good disk-I/O subsystems, the time to unload hundreds of gigabytes to terabytes is both reliable and reasonable. And even though the dump files remain Oracle proprietary, there are also easily identifiable uses of XML within those files. Thus, uncompressed export files are semi-readable within a text editor and can be scanned with operating system commands.

As of Oracle 11g Release 2, the older client based export (i.e. exp) utility will no longer be available or supported. Data Pump Export will become the chief and only method available.

Export Database Level

This is often referred to as a logical backup where physical backup means those performed either via RMAN, operating system commands, or via third party backup and recovery tools. One reason people used logical backup was historically for ease of recovery for when an object was accidentally dropped. However, with Oracle flashback technology, logical backups are becoming far less compelling.

Another reason people performed logical backups was to avoid the perils of the Oracle database migration process when a major new version released. DBAs would simply export the entire database, perform the upgrade, and then import the database.

But over the years the database migration has greatly improved, so this usage has also seen reduced importance. Probably the most prevalent reason for doing logical backups is to provide a simple backup and recovery mechanism with no additional software costs for development and test databases.

```
C:\> expdp bert/bert directory=data_pump_dir dumpfile=logical_backup.dmp
full=y
```

Remember, the user running the data pump export at the database level must have *exp_full_data* privilege for this option to work. Otherwise, the following Oracle errors will be returned:

```
Export: Release 11.1.0.6.0 - Production on Friday, 27 June, 2008 11:20:44

Copyright (c) 2003, 2007, Oracle.  All rights reserved.

Connected to: Oracle Database 11g Enterprise Edition Release 11.1.0.6.0 -
Production

With the Partitioning, OLAP, Data Mining and Real Application Testing
options

ORA-31631: privileges are required

ORA-39161: Full database jobs require privileges
```

Export Tablespace Level

While this may seem like a very useful, and therefore common use case, reality is that often DBAs find that tablespaces are simply containers with space for object allocation. So it is not uncommon over time to find that tablespaces have an eclectic collection of objects. But for those lucky enough and smart enough to have kept some logical rationale to tablespace object placement, here is an example of data pump entirely exporting two specific tablespaces:

```
C:\> expdp bert/bert directory=data_pump_dir dumpfile=multi_tablespace.dmp
tablespaces=users,sysaux
```

One other use for the export at the tablespace level would be if one wished to recreate the tablespace with a different block size such as a tablespace level reorganization. It would be possible to export the tablespace, drop it, recreate it with the new block size, and then import the data. Finally, the tablespace level export can be used as part of the process to merge tablespaces, but that is pretty rare.

As at the database level, the user running the data pump export at the tablespace level must have *exp_full_data* privilege for this option to work if that tablespace contains objects from schemas other than the one running the export. Otherwise, the following Oracle errors will be returned:

```
Export: Release 11.1.0.6.0 - Production on Friday, 27 June, 2008 11:20:44

Copyright (c) 2003, 2007, Oracle.  All rights reserved.

Connected to: Oracle Database 11g Enterprise Edition Release 11.1.0.6.0 -
Production

With the Partitioning, OLAP, Data Mining and Real Application Testing
options

ORA-31631: privileges are required

ORA-39161: Full database jobs require privileges
```

Export Schema Level

There are far too many good reasons to perform data pump exports at the schema level to either explain or justify them all. Suffice it to say that the export of entire schemas is probably one of the most frequently utilized modes. For example, one uses a development database where developers are writing code against a collection of related tables.

Each time a developer runs some code that has yet to pass unit testing, it is possible that the data's ending state may not be entirely consistent, i.e. bug in code may invalidate the data. So the developer needs a way to reset the data between runs. If the DBA makes a schema level data pump export of the base data, then it is a simple procedure to restore the data. Here is an example of exporting two specific schemas:

```
C:\> expdp bert/bert directory=data_pump_dir dumpfile=multi_schema.dmp
schemas=bert,movies
```

Note that when exporting at this level of granularity, the EXCLUDE and INCLUDE options become quite useful. For example, if one wanted to perform that exact same export without corresponding grants, indexes and statistics, here is the additional data pump export syntax required:

```
C:\> expdp bert/bert directory=data_pump_dir dumpfile=schema_exclude.dmp
schemas=bert,movies exclude=grant,index,statistics
```

And if the DBA had instead preferred to only unload those tables and views that started with the string "MOVIE", here is the data pump export command:

```
C:\> expdp bert/bert directory=data_pump_dir dumpfile=schema_include.dmp
schemas=bert,movies include=table:\"like 'MOVIES%'\"
```

Like the database and tablespace levels, the user running the data pump export at the schema level must have *exp_full_data* privilege for this option to work when requesting schemas other than the one running the export.

Export Table Level

Table level data pump export jobs are probably the second most often utilized mode. It is very easy to think in terms of tables when working with data. Table level mode just seems to be the natural granularity of choice. Return to the prior example of the developer working on code who needs the ability to refresh those tables between runs.

The DBA could either export just the tables that developer needs for that programming task, or better yet, the DBA could permit and instruct the developer to export the tables being worked upon. Either way, the data pump export job would work in table mode and for the tables requested, as shown here.

```
C:\> expdp bert/bert directory=data_pump_dir dumpfile=multi_table.dmp
tables=movies.customer,movies.employee
```

Note that the table level mode data pump exports have to be sourced from one schema, or the following error will occur:

```
C:\> expdp bert/bert directory=data_pump_dir dumpfile=multi_table.dmp
tables=movies.customer,movies.employee,bert.junk
```

```
Export: Release 11.1.0.6.0 - Production on Saturday, 28 June, 2008 6:40:21

Copyright (c) 2003, 2007, Oracle.  All rights reserved.

Connected to: Oracle Database 11g Enterprise Edition Release 11.1.0.6.0 -
Production

With the Partitioning, OLAP, Data Mining and Real Application Testing
options

UDE-00012: table mode exports only allow objects from one schema
```

Export Data Subsets

This is probably the most powerful and useful aspect of the data export process, and yet it remains highly underutilized. For instance, it can be used if one wants to extract data from a table by using a filter upon the rows being returned.

That is easily accomplished via a normal *select* command's *where* clause placed in the query parameter passed to the export process. Then one could easily export only those customers who live in Texas as follows:

```
C:\> expdp bert/bert directory=data_pump_dir dumpfile=just_texas.dmp
schemas=movies query=movies.customer:\"where state='TX'\"
```

That seems easy enough – but there is a small catch. The *query* clause is applied to all the tables in the export set, so all the tables better have the columns referenced by that *where* clause. A common example would be a schema table design where each table contains a last modified date column. So if the DBA wanted to unload just records in that schema which had been modified within the past three months, here is the data pump export command for that:

```
C:\>expdp bert/bert directory=data_pump_dir dumpfile=last_mod_date.dmp
schemas=movies query=\"where last_mod_date is not null and last_mod_date >
SYSDATE-90\"
```

Yet as easy and powerful as this method is, there is another method that sometimes can be exactly what one is looking for – the subset by random sample method. If one wanted to export 10% of one's production data for use in development or test environments, then it applies the sample percentage against each object exported.

```
C:\> expdp bert/bert directory=data_pump_dir dumpfile=sample.dmp
schemas=movies sample=10
```

However, there is one major drawback to the sample method: it does not export referentially correct subsets of data. That is because it merely applies a simple algorithm, namely that the percentage represents the probability that a data block of rows will be included in the export's sampling of the data.

This is plainly applied at the table level across all of its data blocks. The sample method does not adhere to any referential integrity constraints or foreign keys defined in the data dictionary. So if an effort to export a 10% sample of the entire schema is made, it will generally end up with messages like those shown below.

```
Processing object type SCHEMA_EXPORT/TABLE/CONSTRAINT/REF_CONSTRAINT

ORA-39083: Object type REF_CONSTRAINT failed to create with error:

ORA-02298: cannot validate (BERT.MOVIETITLE_FK) - parent keys not found
```

Failing SQL is:

```
ALTER TABLE "BERT"."MOVIETITLE" ADD CONSTRAINT "MOVIETITLE_FK" FOREIGN KEY
("CATEGORYID") REFERENCES "BERT"."MOVIECATEGORY" ("CATE

GORYID") ENABLE
```

However, there are ways to get around this. One way could be to create a SQL*Plus script to generate a parameter file with a series of query parameters that would sample the data and retain the foreign key relationships.

But that would constitute a two-step process: run the script to create parameter files and then run the data pump export with no easy way via the database to look at the intermediate results to verify their accuracy before attempting the actual data load.

So instead, the preference is to execute the *extract_data_subset.sql* SQL*Plus script, shown below, to create the subset of the data in a second schema. Then the data can be readily examined for accuracy, and that schema can finally be exported once it is known to be correct.

💾 **extract_data_subset.sql**

```
set linesize 200

set serveroutput on size 100000


create or replace package subsetdata

as

  procedure xgo (xsource varchar2, xtarget varchar2, xpercent integer);

end;

/

show error

create or replace package body subsetdata

as

  type tnames is table of varchar2(32);

  done_arr tnames := tnames();

  done_cnt integer := 0;


  procedure xsample (xsource varchar2, xtarget varchar2, current_table
varchar2, xpercent integer)

  is

    s1   varchar2(256) := 'create table ' || xtarget || '.' || current_table
|| '

as
```

```
select * from ' || xsource || '.' ||current_table;

    s2    varchar2(256) := 'where rownum <= (select ceil(' ||
to_char(xpercent/100) || ' * count(*))

from ' || xsource || '.' || current_table || ');';

    s3    varchar2(256) := 'create table ' || xtarget || '.' || current_table
|| ' as

select T0.* from    ' || xsource || '.' || current_table || ' T0,';

    s4    varchar2(256) := 'where';

    cnt1 integer        := 0;

    cnt2 integer        := 0;

    i    integer        := 0;

    j    integer        := 0;

    es3  varchar2(1)    := '';

    es4  varchar2(4)    := '';

  begin

    i := 0;

    es3 := ',';

    select count(*)

    into cnt1

    from dba_constraints fk,

         dba_constraints pk

    where fk.constraint_type = 'R'

      and fk.owner = xsource

      and fk.R_owner = xsource

      and fk.table_name = current_table

      and pk.constraint_type in ('P','U')

      and pk.owner = xsource

      and pk.table_name != current_table

      and fk.r_constraint_name = pk.constraint_name;

    if (cnt1 = 0) then

    dbms_output.put_line(s1);
```

```
        dbms_output.put_line(s2);
    else
      for c1 in (select pk.table_name,
                        fk.constraint_name fk_name,
                        pk.constraint_name pk_name
                 from dba_constraints fk,
                      dba_constraints pk
                 where fk.constraint_type = 'R'
                   and fk.owner = xsource
                   and fk.R_owner = xsource
                   and fk.table_name = current_table
                   and pk.constraint_type in ('P','U')
                   and pk.owner = xsource
                   and pk.table_name != current_table
                   and fk.r_constraint_name = pk.constraint_name
                ) loop
        i := i + 1;
        if (i = cnt1) then
          es3 := '';
        end if;
        s3 := s3 || '
' || xtarget || '.' || c1.table_name || '  T' || to_char(i) || es3;
        j := 0;
        es4 := ' and';
        select count(*)
        into cnt2
        from dba_cons_columns fk,
             dba_cons_columns pk
        where fk.constraint_name = c1.fk_name
```

```
                and fk.owner = xsource

                and fk.table_name = current_table

                and pk.constraint_name = c1.pk_name

                and pk.owner = xsource

                and pk.table_name != current_table

                and fk.position = pk.position;
         for c2 in (select fk.column_name fk_col,

                          pk.column_name pk_col

                   from dba_cons_columns fk,

                        dba_cons_columns pk

                   where fk.constraint_name = c1.fk_name

                      and fk.owner = xsource

                      and fk.table_name = current_table

                      and pk.constraint_name = c1.pk_name

                      and pk.owner = xsource

                      and pk.table_name != current_table

                      and fk.position = pk.position

                      order by fk.position

                   ) loop

          j := j + 1;

          if (i = cnt1) and (j = cnt2) then

            es4 := ';';

          end if;

          s4 := s4 || '
' || 'T0.' || c2.fk_col || ' = T' || to_char(i) || '.' || c2.pk_col || es4;
        end loop;

      end loop;

    dbms_output.put_line(s3);

    dbms_output.put_line(s4);

   end if;
```

```
   done_arr.extend(1);

   done_cnt := done_cnt+1;

   done_arr(done_cnt) := current_table;

 end;


 procedure xprocess (xsource varchar2, xtarget varchar2, current_table
varchar2, xpercent integer)
 is
   i    integer := 1;

   flg  integer := 1;

   cnt1 integer := 0;

   cnt2 integer := 0;
 begin
   xsample (xsource, xtarget, current_table, xpercent);

   for c1 in (select fk.table_name

               from dba_constraints fk,

                    dba_constraints pk

               where fk.constraint_type = 'R'

                 and fk.owner = xsource

                 and fk.R_owner = xsource

                 and fk.table_name != current_table

                 and pk.constraint_type in ('P','U')

                 and pk.owner = xsource

                 and pk.table_name = current_table

                 and fk.r_constraint_name = pk.constraint_name

              ) loop

      select count(*)

      into cnt1

      from dba_constraints fk,

           dba_constraints pk
```

```
          where fk.constraint_type = 'R'
            and fk.owner = xsource
            and fk.R_owner = xsource
            and fk.table_name = c1.table_name
            and pk.constraint_type in ('P','U')
            and pk.owner = xsource
            and pk.table_name != current_table
            and fk.r_constraint_name = pk.constraint_name;
   if (cnt1 > 0) then
     cnt2 := 0;
     flg  := 0;
     for c2 in (select pk.table_name
                  from dba_constraints fk,
                       dba_constraints pk
                  where fk.constraint_type = 'R'
                    and fk.owner = xsource
                    and fk.R_owner = xsource
                    and fk.table_name = c1.table_name
                    and pk.constraint_type in ('P','U')
                    and pk.owner = xsource
                    and pk.table_name != current_table
                    and fk.r_constraint_name = pk.constraint_name
               ) loop
       i := 1;
       while (i <= done_cnt) loop
         if (c2.table_name = done_arr(i)) then
           cnt2 := cnt2 + 1;
         end if;
         i := i + 1;
```

```
          end loop;

      end loop;

      if (cnt1 = cnt2) then

        flg := 1;

      end if;

    end if;

    if (flg = 1) then

      xprocess (xsource, xtarget, c1.table_name, xpercent);

    end if;

  end loop;

end;


procedure xgo (xsource varchar2, xtarget varchar2, xpercent integer)

is

begin

  for c1 in (select table_name

            from dba_tables tab

            where tab.owner = xsource

              and NOT EXISTS (select 1

                            from dba_constraints fk

                            where fk.constraint_type = 'R'

                              and fk.owner = xsource

                              and fk.R_owner = xsource

                              and fk.table_name = tab.table_name

                          )

          ) loop

    xprocess (xsource, xtarget, c1.table_name, xpercent);

  end loop;

end;

end;
```

```
/

show error


prompt

###

###   subsetdata.xgo(SOURCE_SCHEMA,TARGET_SCHEMA,PERCENTAGE)

###

exec subsetdata.xgo('MOVIES','BERT',10)
```

Looking at the last statement in the *extract_data_subset.sql* SQL*Plus script, simply call the *subsetdata.xgo* procedure to run, thereby specifying the source and target schemas, plus the sampling percentage. The *extract_data_subset.sql* SQL*Plus script walks the database referential integrity dependency tree and maintains it for the data sample being generated. The *extract_data_subset.sql* output, shown next, is an example of the generated script for copying 10% of the simple MOVIES demo schema copied to the BERT intermediate schema.

```
extract_data_subset.sql output


create table BERT.CUSTOMER

as

select * from MOVIES.CUSTOMER

where rownum <= (select ceil(.1 * count(*))

from MOVIES.CUSTOMER);


create table BERT.EMPLOYEE

as

select * from MOVIES.EMPLOYEE

where rownum <= (select ceil(.1 * count(*))

from MOVIES.EMPLOYEE);
```

```
create table BERT.MOVIERENTAL as

select T0.* from   MOVIES.MOVIERENTAL  T0,

 BERT.CUSTOMER   T1,

 BERT.EMPLOYEE   T2

where

 T0.CUSTOMERID = T1.CUSTOMERID and

 T0.EMPLOYEEID = T2.EMPLOYEEID;


create table BERT.MOVIECATEGORY

as

select * from MOVIES.MOVIECATEGORY

where rownum <= (select ceil(.1 * count(*))

from MOVIES.MOVIECATEGORY);


create table BERT.MOVIETITLE as

select T0.* from   MOVIES.MOVIETITLE  T0,

 BERT.MOVIECATEGORY   T1

where

 T0.CATEGORYID = T1.CATEGORYID;


create table BERT.MOVIECOPY as

select T0.* from   MOVIES.MOVIECOPY  T0,

 BERT.MOVIETITLE   T1

where

 T0.MOVIEID = T1.MOVIEID;


create table BERT.RENTALITEM as

select T0.* from   MOVIES.RENTALITEM  T0,
```

```
 BERT.MOVIERENTAL  T1,

 BERT.MOVIECOPY  T2
where
 T0.RENTALID = T1.RENTALID and

 T0.MOVIECOPYID = T2.MOVIECOPYID;
```

Now the data can be verified as correct using standard SQL *select* commands and then export that data using the data pump export at the schema level. Although this method requires a little additional database disk space to build the subset data, disk space is so cheap and this method provides a simple method for examining intermediate results. Since it maintains referential integrity, it is obviously superior to the data pump export sample method.

The Windows Script for Export

This next script runs an Oracle Data Pump Export using a parameter file. It also accomplishes the following:

- Rotates the filenames to keep two copies and avoid the "output file exists" error. The .* is used as the extension so both the logfiles and dumpfiles are renamed.

- Searches the logfile to determine if there are any errors using the *findstr* command.

- Uses the *blat* utility to send an email upon completion.

The extra steps can be stripped out if you do not need the emails sent, the files renamed, or the logs scanned. Note the use of the *goto*.

🖫 **Data_pump_export_oracle_windows.bat**

```
::
::   expdp_orcl.bat
::
::   exports orcl database and emails results using DATAPUMP
::
```

```
::   save 2 revs
::
del d:\exports\expdp_orcl2.*

ren d:\exports\expdp_orcl1.*  expdp_orcl2.*
ren d:\exports\expdp_orcl.*  expdp_orcl1.*

set oracle_sid=orcl

expdp "'/ as sysdba'" parfile=c:\adminscripts\exports\expdp_orcl.par

::
:: check for completion with or without warnings
::

findstr /C:"successfully completed" d:\exports\expdp_orcl.log  && goto next1
findstr /C:"error" d:\exports\expdp_orcl.log  && goto next2
Blat d:\exports\expdp_orcl.log  -t dba@email.com -s "Export failed"
goto eof

:next1
Blat d:\exports\expdp_orcl.log  -t dba@email.com -s "Export completed"
goto eof

:next2
Blat d:\exports\expdp_orcl.log  -t dba@email.com -s "Export error"

:eof
Exit

EXPDP_ORCL.PAR contents
logfile=expdp_orcl.log
dumpfile=expdp_orcl.dmp
directory=datapump_dir
full=Y
```

Next, let's examine how we can parse our alert log file to extract errors in Windows.

Check Oracle Alert Logs for ORA-

This next script scans the Oracle Alert Log for the string ORA- and sends email if it is found. Rather than emailing the entire alert log, it has logic to strip the first ORA- error it finds and sends that. If it does not find ORA-, then it drops to the next line, which sends it to the *eof* tag to exit.

You can write a DOS batch file to check the Oracle Alert Log. This Windows alert log check script is simple. Like the UNIX scripts, it parses for alert log messages, but instead of using *grep*, it uses the DOS *findstr* command.

In this example, we locate all error messages, those beginning with ORA-, and direct the result to a temp directory for more detailed analysis:

```
findstr "ORA-" c:\oracle\admin\MYSID\bdump\alert_MYSID.log >
c:\tmp\error.txt
```

You can easily monitor the Oracle alert log for error messages and send those messages to the DBA via email. The Oracle Windows *bat* file below reads the alert log using the following logic flow:

- Reads the alert log extracting all of the Oracle error messages into an *alert_log_err.txt* file

- Compares the *alert_log_err.txt* file to a file containing previously extracted errors (*alert_log_old.txt*)

- Sends any differences (new errors) to the DBA via email

🖫 examine_errors_alert_log_oracle_windows.bat

```
@ECHO OFF
REM +---------------------------------
REM |   ALERT_LOG.BAT
REM +------------------------------------
REM | Set up client specific variables
REM +------------------------------------

set BC_DIR=C:\BC
set FROM=Oracle@Client.com
set TO=Client@remote-dba.net
set SUBJECT=Client Alert Log

set ORACLE_SID=MYDB
set ORACLE_BASE=C:\ORACLE
set ORACLE_HOME=C:\ORACLE\ORA102

REM +----------------------------------------------------------------
REM | Now let's go get all the errors from the Alert Log
REM +----------------------------------------------------------------
```

```
egrep -h -e ORA- -e Errors
%ORACLE_BASE%\admin\%ORACLE_SID%\bdump\ALERT_%ORACLE_SID%.LOG >
alert_log_err.txt

REM +------------------------------------------------------------
REM | If we don't have an old file to compare with, then
REM | create the old file
REM +------------------------------------------------------------

if exist %BC_DIR%\Report\alert_log_old.txt goto COMPARE
touch %BC_DIR%\Report\alert_log_old.txt

:COMPARE
REM +------------------------------------------------------------
REM | Compare the errors that we got this time with errors we
REM | got last time, keeping only new errors.
REM +------------------------------------------------------------

comm -23 alert_log_err.txt %BC_DIR%\Report\alert_log_old.txt > To_e-Mail.txt

:MOVE
REM +------------------------------------------------------------
REM | Save all the current errors for next time.
REM +------------------------------------------------------------

mv alert_log_err.txt %BC_DIR%\Report\alert_log_old.txt

REM +------------------------------------------------------------
REM | If new errors then e-mail them else exit
REM +------------------------------------------------------------

getlines 1 1 To_e-mail.txt > del.it
if errorlevel 1 goto END

REM +------------------------------------------------------------
REM | Mail the Alert Log to the DBA staff
REM +------------------------------------------------------------

banner Alert Log > message.txt
echo. >> message.txt
udate >> message.txt
echo. >> message.txt
cat message.txt To_e-mail.txt >> xxx.txt

sendmail -messagefile=xxx.txt -from=%FROM% -subject="%SUBJECT%" %TO%

:END
rm -s del.it
rm -s message.txt
rm -s To_e-mail.txt
rm -s xxx.txt

exit
```

This is extremely useful for other things, such as scanning application logs for particular errors or strings and reporting when they are found.

Ideally, such a script would run as a recurring Windows Scheduled Task at an interval of however often you wish to check, such as every 10 minutes or every hour.

🖫 **check_alert_log_oracle_windows.bat**

```
::
:: check_alert.bat
::
:: checks for ORA errors in alert log and emails them off
::
:: look for ORA- in alertlog. If found call send_mail routine else drop thru
:: to next line which is a goto the eof tag
::
@findstr "ORA-" C:\oracle10g\admin\orcl\bdump\alert_orcl.log && call
:send_mail
goto :eof

:: Subroutine to send mail

:send_mail
del /Q c:\adminscripts\checkdb\error.txt

find "ORA-" < C:\oracle10g\admin\orcl\bdump\alert_orcl.log >
c:\adminscripts\checkdb\error.txt

Blat  c:\adminscripts\checkdb\error.txt -t dba@email.com -s "ORCL error"

goto :eof

:eof
Exit
```

Checking for a Running Service

This next script does a *net start* command to list the services, places the output into a file, and then scans the file for whatever service you care to verify is running – in this case, OracleServiceORCL.

If it is not found, then an email is sent to the Oracle DBA using the *blat* utility. In addition, one could do a *net start* to restart the service, if desired, to minimize downtime.

This is useful for checking services besides Oracle related ones, and can be very useful for troublesome Windows services that are part of

Vendor Applications that sometimes die for no apparent reason; this one may save you a 3:00 AM phone call!

💾 verify_running_oracle_windows.bat

```
::   check_DBSvc.cmd
::
::   checks to be sure DB Service is running
::
::   Delete workfile, Look for DB service from NET START command
::   If we find it, just exit, else send mail
::
del /Q c:\adminscripts\uptime\services.txt
net start > c:\adminscripts\uptime\services.txt

findstr /C:"OracleServiceORCL" c:\adminscripts\uptime\services.txt && goto
:eof

::
::   didn't find service, so drop thru to here and send mail
::

:send_mail
Blat  c:\adminscripts\uptime\services.txt -t DBA@email.com -s "ORCL DB
Service not running "
goto :eof

::
::   The End
::
:eof
exit
```

Clear Out Excess Archivelog Files

This next script deletes archivelogs that are over 7 days old. This can of course be adjusted to as many days as you wish. It also does a directory before and after, so it would be handy to direct the output of the scheduled task to a file in order to see the before and after.

💾 clean_archives.bat

```
::
::   clean_archives.bat
::
::   simple script, deletes archivelogs over 7 days old
::

:: Get rid of files using forfiles utility
```

```
dir d:\oracle\oradata\orcl\archives

forfiles /p d:\oracle\oradata\orcl\archives /m *.* /d -7 -c "cmd /c del/q
@FILE"

dir d:\oracle\oradata\orcl\archives

exit
```

Clear Out Old RMAN Backup Files

This script deletes RMAN backup files that are over 3 days old and
sends an email when done. It does before and after directories, and runs
the after directory to a file, which then gets emailed. Again, the number
of days can be adjusted to whatever you have space to keep.

🖫 **clean_rman_oracle_windows.bat**

```
::
::   clean_RMAN.bat
::
::   simple script, deletes RMANs over 3 days old
::

dir D:\oracle\oradata\orcl\rman

forfiles /p D:\oracle\oradata\orcl\rman /m * /d -3 -c "cmd /c del/q @FILE"

dir D:\oracle\oradata\orcl\rman >
C:\Adminscripts\maint\RMAN_current_list.txt

Blat c:\adminscripts\maint\RMAN_current_list.txt -tf
C:\Adminscripts\oracle_dba_email_info.txt -s "RMAN Purge complete"
```

Purge Audit Tables

This script calls a SQL script that purges the Oracle Audit Table AUD$.
This is an important example because it demonstrates how you can
execute Oracle SQL commands from a Windows batch job.

🖫 **purge_audit_tables_oracle_windows.bat**

```
::
::   clear_audit.bat
```

```
::
::   Clears Oracle Audit table - calls clear_audit.sql
::
:: Set oracle sid

set oracle_sid=ORCL

:: Delete previous log file

del /Q c:\adminscripts\maint\purge_audit.log

::Call SQL*Plus and execute the clear_audit script

SQL*Plus /nolog @c:\adminscripts\maint\purge_audit.sql

:: Email results

Blat  c:\adminscripts\maint\purge_audit.log -t dba@email.com -s "ORCL Clear
Audit Log"
```

clear_audit.sql contents:

```
connect / as sysdba
set pagesize 0
set linesize 1000
set echo on
alter session set nls_date_format = 'YYYY-MM-DD:HH24:MI:SS';
spool c:\adminscripts\maint\clear_audit.log
select count (*) from aud$;
select count(*) from aud$ where ntimestamp# < sysdate-100;
delete from aud$ where ntimestamp# < sysdate-100;
select count(*) from aud$;
commit;
set echo off
spool off
exit
```

Oracle Cold Backups on Windows

Cold backup using scripts can back up an Oracle database whether it is in ARCHIVELOG mode or not. A cold backup means that the database is shutdown, and all files are backed up via a manually created script.

Generally speaking, the DBA can always recover from a cold backup unless something happens to the backup media or files. However, unless

---

the database is in ARCHIVELOG mode, a cold backup is a point-in-time backup.

If a database is archive logging, which means that all filled redo logs are copied to an archive log before being reused, the cold backup can be restored to the server and archive logs applied to make the database as nearly current as possible.

The drawbacks to cold backups are that the database must be shut down in order to perform a cold backup, a cold backup can take a long period of time depending on database size, and the DBA has to manually maintain the backup scripts. Another problem is that cold backup on raw partitions on UNIX or Linux involves the command *dd*. Cold backup, by its very nature, defeats the purpose of a high availability 24x7 RAC database solution.

Normal system backups, referred to as either hot or cold backups, are used to protect the system from media failure. Each can and should be used when required.

A cold backup, that is, one done with the database in a shutdown state, provides a complete copy of the database that can be restored exactly. The generalized procedure for using a cold backup is as follows:

1. Using the shutdown script(s) provided, shutdown the Oracle instance(s) to be backed up.

2. Ensure that there is enough backup media to back up the entire database. Mount the first volume of the backup media (9 track, WORM, 4mm, 8mm, etc.) using the proper operating system *mount* command.

3. Issue the proper Operating System backup command to initiate the backup.

4. Once the backup is complete, be sure all backup volumes are properly labeled and stored, away from the computer.

5. The final volume is dismounted from the tape drive using the appropriate operating system *dismount* command.

6. Restart the Oracle instances using the appropriate startup script(s).

This next script is a bit more complex. It stops the Oracle service and the listener, deletes the previous backup files, copies the datafiles and redo logs, etc. to backup directories, and restarts the listener and database.

The font was shrunk on the *xcopy* commands so all the code would fit on the same line.

🖫 cold_backup_oracle_windows.bat

```
::
:: OracleColdBackup.bat
::
:: This script is used to stop Oracle Instance and Services, copy the
:: files off to disk, and restart the database prior to tape backup
::
echo on
::
:: delete last night's copy
::
rmdir /s /Q d:\oracle\saves\c
rmdir /s /Q d:\oracle\saves\d
rmdir /s /Q d:\oracle\saves\e
::
:: stop listener service
::
net stop OracleOraDb10g_home1TNSListener
::
::  shutdown database
::
::
net stop OracleServiceORCL
::
::  wait 60 seconds
::
ping -n 60 127.0.0.1>nul
::
::  copy files
::
xcopy /c /f /e /y /k /o c:\oracle\oradata\* d:\oracle\saves\c\oracle\oradata\*
xcopy /c /f /e /y /k /o d:\oracle\oradata\* d:\oracle\saves\d\oracle\oradata\*
xcopy /c /f /e /y /k /o e:\oracle\oradata\* d:\oracle\saves\e\oracle\oradata\*
xcopy /c /f /e /y /k /o c:\oracle\admin\ORCL\* d:\oracle\saves\c\oracle\admin\ORCL\*
xcopy /c /f /e /y /k /o d:\oracle\10g\database\* d:\oracle\saves\d\oracle\10g\database\*
::
::  start database
```

```
::
::
net start OracleServiceORCL
::
:: wait 10 seconds
::
ping -n 10 127.0.0.1>nul
::
:: start Listener
::
net start OracleOraDb10g_home1TNSListener
::
:: done
::
exit
```

Script to Report on Blocking Sessions

Sadly, Oracle time-series tables (STATSPACK and AWR) do not track blocking session and waiting sessions, but the extra-cost ASH components can track blocking sessions for one hour into the past.

As a blocking session alert mechanism, you can schedule a job to check every 5 minutes for a blocking session (using this script to find blocking sessions with *v$session*) and then trigger a procedure to locate the exact data block where the blocking/waiting occurred. This automated blocking tracing can then be emailed to the DBA for subsequent investigation and repair.

Here is a query that gives us a list of blocking sessions and the sessions that they are blocking:

```
select
   blocking_session,
   sid,
   serial#,
   wait_class,
   seconds_in_wait
from
   v$session
where
   blocking_session is not NULL
order by
   blocking_session;

BLOCKING_SESSION        SID     SERIAL# WAIT_CLASS            SECONDS_IN_WAIT
----------------- ---------- ---------- -------------------- --------
              148        135      61521 Idle                              64
```

In this case, we find that session 148 is blocking session 135 and has been for 64 seconds.

This batch job runs a SQL*Plus script to check the database for Blocking Sessions, and sends an email if any are found. There is also a section that checks the time of day, so it does not send alerts between 10:00 PM and 5:59 AM. This can be done in any script if there are times you wish to not run the commands.

💾 report_blocking_sessions_oracle_windows.bat

```
::    checks for blocking sessions
::

::
::    Check the time and exit if 10pm to 5:59am
::

del /Q c:\adminscripts\lockscan\time.txt
@echo %time:~0,2% > c:\adminscripts\lockscan\time.txt
findstr /C:"22" c:\adminscripts\lockscan\time.txt && goto :eof
findstr /C:"23" c:\adminscripts\lockscan\time.txt && goto :eof
findstr /C:" 1" c:\adminscripts\lockscan\time.txt && goto :eof
findstr /C:" 2" c:\adminscripts\lockscan\time.txt && goto :eof
findstr /C:" 3" c:\adminscripts\lockscan\time.txt && goto :eof
findstr /C:" 4" c:\adminscripts\lockscan\time.txt && goto :eof
findstr /C:" 5" c:\adminscripts\lockscan\time.txt && goto :eof

::
::    do query for blocking sessions and spool to logfile
::

set oracle_sid=orcl

SQL*Plus "/ as sysdba" @c:\adminscripts\lockscan\lock_scan.sql

::
::    look for 'no rows selected' and if found goto exit
::

@findstr /c:"no rows selected" c:\adminscripts\lockscan\locks.txt && goto
:eof

::
::    If no rows selected not found, we have a blocking lock - send email and
exit
::

:send_mail

Blat  c:\adminscripts\lockscan\locks.txt -tf
c:\adminscripts\lockscan\emails.txt -s "ORCL Blocking Session"
```

```
::
:: Exit
::

:eof

exit
```

Contents of 'lock_scan.sql' file

```
spool c:\adminscripts\lockscan\locks.txt

select
   blocking_session,
   sid,
   serial#,
   wait_class,
   seconds_in_wait
from
   v$session
where
   blocking_session is not NULL
order by
   blocking_session;

spool off

exit
```

Killing an Oracle Blocking Session

This script will query the *dba_lock* and *dba_blockers* view to locate a blocking session:

```
COLUMN username          FORMAT a10 HEADING 'Holding|User'
COLUMN session_id                   HEADING 'SID'
COLUMN mode_held         FORMAT a20 HEADING 'Mode|Held'
COLUMN mode_requested    FORMAT a20 HEADING 'Mode|Requested'
COLUMN lock_id1          FORMAT a20 HEADING 'Lock|ID1'
COLUMN lock_id2          FORMAT a20 HEADING 'Lock|ID2'
COLUMN type                         HEADING 'Lock|Type'
SET LINES 132 PAGES 59 FEEDBACK OFF ECHO OFF
START title132 'Sessions Blocking Other Sessions Report'
SPOOL rep_out\&db\blockers
SELECT
      a.session_id,
      username,
      type,
      mode_held,
```

```
      mode_requested,
      lock_id1,
      lock_id2
FROM
      sys.v_$session b,
      sys.dba_blockers c,
      sys.dba_lock a
WHERE
      c.holding_session=a.session_id and
      c.holding_session=b.sid
/
SPOOL OFF
PAUSE press enter/return to continue
CLEAR COLUMNS
SET LINES 80 PAGES 22 FEEDBACK ON ECHO ON
```

Example script to report on blocking locks:

```
rem
rem FUNCTION: Report on sessions waiting for locks
rem
COLUMN busername FORMAT A10 HEADING 'Holding|User'
COLUMN wusername FORMAT A10 HEADING 'Waiting|User'
COLUMN bsession_id HEADING 'Holding|Sid'
COLUMN wsession_id HEADING 'Waiting|Sid'
COLUMN mode_held FORMAT A20 HEADING 'Mode|Held'
COLUMN mode_requested FORMAT A20 HEADING 'Mode|Requested'
COLUMN lock_id1 FORMAT A20 HEADING 'Lock|Id1'
COLUMN lock_id2 FORMAT A20 HEADING 'Lock|Id2'
COLUMN type HEADING 'LOCK|TYPE'
SET LINES 132 PAGES 59 FEEDBACK OFF ECHO OFF
START TITLE132 'Processes Waiting on Locks Report'
SPOOL rep_out/&db/waiters
SELECT
      holding_session bsession_id,
      waiting_session wsession_id,
      b.username busername,
      a.username wusername,
      c.lock_type type,
      mode_held, mode_requested,
      lock_id1, lock_id2
FROM
sys.v_$session b, sys.dba_waiters c, sys.v_$session a
WHERE
c.holding_session=b.sid and
c.waiting_session=a.sid
/
SPOOL OFF
PAUSE press enter/return to continue
CLEAR COLUMNS
SET LINES 80 PAGES 22 FEEDBACK ON ECHO ON
TTITLE OFF
```

Example output from the blockers report is shown for a simple lock
situation:

```
Date: 02/08/00                                                           Page:    1
Time: 07:01 AM            Sessions Blocking Other Sessions Report        SYSTEM
                                 aultdb database


          Holding    Lock     Mode       Mode         Lock            Lock
    SID   User       Type     Held       Requested    ID1             ID2
--------- ---------- -------- ---------- ------------ --------------- ----
      9   LABUSER    USER     Row-X (SX) None         2821            0
      9   LABUSER    USER     Exclusive  None         196702          5547
```

The output for the same lock situation from the waiters report is shown:

```
Date:02/08/00
                                          Page:   1
Time: 07:01 AM                Processes Waiting on Locks Report
SYSTEM
                                     aultdb database

  Holding   Waiting Holding  Waiting   Lock       ModMode         Lock
Lock
     SID        SID User     User      Type       Held            Requested      ID1
ID2
--------- --------- ---------- ----------- ------------ --------------------- --------------------- ---
--------------------- -----------
        9        13 LABUSER   LABUSER2  Transaction Exclusive       Exclusive
196702          5547
```

Next, let's see how to make a *bat* file to collect CBO statistics.Oracle
Statistics Script for Windows

The term "Oracle statistics" may refer to historical performance statistics
that are kept in STATSPACK and AWR, but a more common use of the
term "Oracle statistics" is about Oracle optimizer "Metadata statistics",
information that provides the cost-based SQL optimizer with the
information about the nature of the tables and indexes.

Oracle statistics tell you the size of the tables, the distribution of values
within a column, and other important information so that SQL
statements will always generate the "best" execution plans.

The most important key to success with the cost-based SQL optimizer
(CBO) is to carefully define and manage your statistics. In order for the
CBO to make an intelligent decision about the best execution plan for
your SQL, it must have information about the table and indexes that
participate in the query. When the CBO knows the size of the tables
and the distribution, cardinality, and selectivity of column values, the
CBO can make an informed decision and almost always generates the
best execution plan.

Tips for Optimizing the CBO with Statistics

There are several tips for optimizing your CBO with good statistics:

- **Find skewed columns that are referenced in SQL**: Many shops do not use method_opt=skewonly and suffer from poor execution plans on skewed column access.

- **Find histograms for foreign key columns**: Many DBAs forget that the CBO must have foreign-key histograms in order to determine the optimal table join order (i.e. the ORDERED hint).

- **Fix the cause, not the symptom**: For example, whenever there is a sub-optimal order for table joins, resist the temptation to add the ORDERED hint and instead create histograms on the foreign keys of the join to force the CBO to make the best decision.

As a review, the CBO gathers information from many sources, and has the lofty goal of using DBA-provided metadata to always make the "best" execution plan decision.

Oracle uses data from many sources to make an execution plan (Figure 13.1)

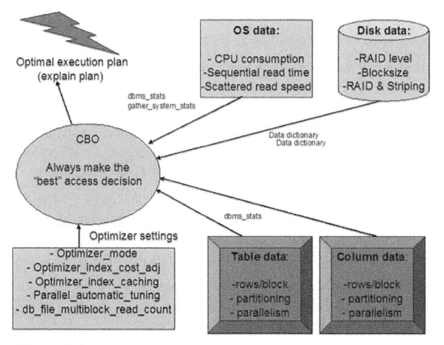

Figure 13.1: *Factors influencing SQL execution in Windows*

Let's examine the following areas of CBO statistics and see how to gather top-quality statistics for the CBO and how to create an appropriate CBO environment for your database.

Getting Top-Quality Statistics for the CBO

The choices of executions plans made by the CBO are only as good as the statistics available to it. The old-fashioned analyze table and *dbms_utility* methods for generating CBO statistics are obsolete and somewhat dangerous to SQL performance. As we may know, the CBO uses object statistics to choose the best execution plan for all SQL statements.

The *dbms_stats* utility does a far better job in estimating statistics, especially for large partitioned tables, and the better statistics result in faster SQL execution plans. Here is a sample execution of *dbms_stats* with the OPTIONS clause:

```
exec dbms_stats.gather_schema_stats( -
   ownname          => 'SCOTT', -
   options          => 'GATHER AUTO', -
   estimate_percent => dbms_stats.auto_sample_size, -
   method_opt       => 'for all columns size repeat', -
   degree           => 34 -
   )
```

Here is another *dbms_stats* example that creates histograms on all indexes columns:

```
BEGIN
dbms_stats.gather_schema_stats(
ownname=>'TPCC',
METHOD_OPT=>'FOR ALL INDEXED COLUMNS SIZE SKEWONLY',
CASCADE=>TRUE,
ESTIMATE_PERCENT=>100);
END;
/
```

There are several values for the OPTIONS parameter that we need to know about:

- GATHER_ reanalyzes the whole schema

- GATHER EMPTY_ only analyzes tables that have no existing statistics

- GATHER STALE_ only reanalyzes tables with more than 10 percent modifications (inserts, updates, deletes).

- GATHER AUTO_ will reanalyze objects that currently have no statistics and objects with stale statistics. Using GATHER AUTO is like combining GATHER STALE and GATHER EMPTY.

Note that both GATHER STALE and GATHER AUTO require monitoring. If you issue the ALTER TABLE XXX MONITORING command, Oracle tracks changed tables with the *dba_tab_modifications* view. Below we see that the exact number of inserts, updates, and deletes are tracked since the last analysis of statistics:

```
SQL> desc dba_tab_modifications;

Name                     Type
-------------------------------------------
TABLE_OWNER              VARCHAR2(30)
TABLE_NAME               VARCHAR2(30)
PARTITION_NAME           VARCHAR2(30)
SUBPARTITION_NAME        VARCHAR2(30)
INSERTS                  NUMBER
UPDATES                  NUMBER
DELETES                  NUMBER
TIMESTAMP                DATE
TRUNCATED                VARCHAR2(3)
```

The most interesting of these options is the GATHER STALE option. Because all statistics will become stale quickly in a robust OLTP database, we must remember the rule for GATHER STALE is > 10% row change (based on *num_rows* at statistics collection time).

Hence, almost every table except read-only tables will be reanalyzed with the GATHER STALE option, making the GATHER STALE option best for systems that are largely read-only. For example, if only five percent of the database tables get significant updates, then only five percent of the tables will be reanalyzed with the GATHER STALE option.

Automating Sample Size with *dbms_stats*

The better the quality of the statistics, the better the job that the CBO will do when determining your execution plans. Unfortunately, doing a complete analysis on a large database could take days, and most shops must sample your database to get CBO statistics. The goal is to take a large enough sample of the database to provide top-quality data for the CBO.

Now that we see how the *dbms_stats* option works, let's see how to specify an adequate sample size for *dbms_stats*.

In earlier releases, the DBA had to guess what percentage of the database provided the best sample size and sometimes under-analyzed the schema. Starting with Oracle9i Database, the *estimate_percent* argument is a great way to allow Oracle's *dbms_stats* to automatically estimate the "best" percentage of a segment to sample when gathering statistics:

```
estimate_percent => dbms_stats.auto_sample_size
```

After collecting automatic sample sizes, you can verify the accuracy of the automatic statistics sampling by looking at the *sample_size* column on any of these data dictionary views:

```
DBA_ALL_TABLES
DBA_INDEXES
DBA_IND_PARTITIONS
DBA_IND_SUBPARTITIONS
DBA_OBJECT_TABLES
DBA_PART_COL_STATISTICS
DBA_SUBPART_COL_STATISTICS
DBA_TABLES
DBA_TAB_COLS
DBA_TAB_COLUMNS
DBA_TAB_COL_STATISTICS
DBA_TAB_PARTITIONS
DBA_TAB_SUBPARTITIONS
```

Note that Oracle generally chooses a *sample_size* from 5 to 20 percent when using automatic sampling, depending on the size of the tables and the distribution of column values. Remember, the better the quality of your statistics, the better the decision of the CBO.

This script calls a SQL script to estimate statistics on the database. This is another example that demonstrates how you can execute Oracle SQL commands from a Windows batch job.

estimate_optimizer_statistics_oracle_windows.bat

```
::
::    stats.bat
::
::    Estimates statistics
```

```
:: Set oracle sid

set oracle_sid=ORCL

:: Get rid of previous log file

del /Q c:\adminscripts\stats\analyze_ORCL.log

SQL*Plus "/ as sysdba" @c:\adminscripts\stats\stats.sql

::
:: Email results
::

Blat  c:\adminscripts\stats\analyze_ORCL.log -t dba@email.com -s "ORCL Prod
Analyze Logfile"

Exit
```

stats.sql contents:

```
set trimspool on
set echo on
column name new_value db_name noprint
select name from v$database;

spool c:\adminscripts\stats\analyze_&db_name..log

prompt Estimating Statistics for Tables/Indexes...

select to_char(sysdate, 'DD-MON-YYYY HH24:MI:SS') as start_time from dual;

exec
dbms_stats.gather_database_stats(estimate_percent=>dbms_stats.auto_sample_si
ze, method_opt=>'FOR ALL COLUMNS SIZE AUTO', cascade=>true, options=>'GATHER
AUTO');

select to_char(sysdate, 'DD-MON-YYYY HH24:MI:SS') as stop_time from dual;

exec dbms_stats.alter_database_tab_monitoring;

spool off
exit;
```

Next, let's look at a script that can be used to check for disk free space.

Batch File for Checking Oracle Windows Disk Free Space

You can easily monitor Oracle Windows disk space usage with a Windows script that monitors disk free space. If a disk volume has less free space than a pre-determined threshold, an alert message is sent to the DBA via email using the *disk_space.bat* script.

🖫 disk_space.bat

```
@ECHO OFF

REM +-----------------------------------
REM | DISK_SPACE.BAT
REM +-----------------------------------
REM | Set up client specific variables
REM +-----------------------------------

set BC_DIR=C:\BC

REM +------------------------------------------------------------
REM | Define minimum space value in floating point format
REM | Example: 1E5=100,000 (100K)    1.75E5=175,000 (175K)
REM |          2E6=2,000,000 (2MB)
REM +------------------------------------------------------------
set MINSPACE=1.75E5

ucd %BC_DIR%\script

REM +------------------------------------------------------------
REM | Now let's go get disk space information for all disks and
REM | remove commas from the byte values
REM +------------------------------------------------------------

df -a -t | sed -e "s/,//g" > df.txt

REM +------------------------------------------------------------
REM | Select lines for disks that fall within the critical free
REM | space range and send them to the ALERT.TXT file
REM +------------------------------------------------------------

getrng "-d)" -f2 -r 0,%MINSPACE% df.txt > alert.txt

REM +------------------------------------------------------------
REM | If we found disks critically low on space, send an e-mail
REM | alert to the DBA staff
REM +------------------------------------------------------------

test -s1 alert.txt    run: sendalrt.bat alert.txt

rm -s df.txt
rm -s alert.txt
```

```
REM +-------------------------------------
REM | Set up client specific variables
REM +-------------------------------------

set FROM=Oracle@Client.com
set TO=Client@remote-dba.net
set SUBJECT=Client Freespace Alert

REM +-------------------------------------
REM | Build the message banner
REM +-------------------------------------

echo. > message.txt
banner Disk Alert! >> message.txt
echo. >> message.txt

cat message.txt %1% >> combined.txt

REM +-------------------------------------
REM | Send the alert message
REM +-------------------------------------

sendmail -messagefile=combined.txt -subject="%SUBJECT%" -from=%FROM%   %TO%

rm message.txt
rm combined.txt
exit


exit
```

Finally, let's take a look at the *sendmail* program.

Sending an Email from an Oracle Windows Script

The following Windows *bat* file code demonstrates how the *sendmail* program is invoked from Windows. This program accepts the report file name as an argument (for instance a SQL*PLUS spooled file) which it uses in the *–attach* parameter of the *sendmail* program.

The *sendmail* recipient (TO), sender (FROM), and subject information are set up as variables in the Windows *bat* file to facilitate the use of the batch program on different servers and in different sites. In the

Windows *bat* files, the *sendmail* message text is generated dynamically using echo statements.

```
@ECHO OFF

REM +----------------------------------
REM | Set up client specific variables
REM +----------------------------------

set BC_DIR=C:\BC
set FROM=Oracle@Client.com
set TO=Client@remote-dba.net
set SUBJECT=*** Client TRACE ALERT

set FILENAME=%1

  .
  .
  .
  .
REM +-------------------------------------------------------------
REM | Build message text
REM +-------------------------------------------------------------

echo. > message.txt
echo 'Please see attached dump identified on' >> message.txt
udate >> message.txt

sendmail -messagefile=message.txt -from=%FROM% -subject="%SUBJECT%" -
attach=%FILENAME%  %TO%

:END
rm -s message.txt
rm -s %FILENAME%
```

Summary

This chapter has demonstrated how many common DBA tasks such as backups, exports, log checking, file cleanup, and many more can be automated via Windows Scripts.

These are just some examples of what can be done. Expand on them and with some research and ingenuity, you can do many tasks this way.

Now we are ready to move on and examine some miscellaneous items that relate to running Oracle on Windows.

Miscellaneous Things That Had No Category

Introduction

The following few items were added here because there was no category to create an entire chapter on, but they are useful enough to warrant mention! Included in this chapter are several useful commands and tips that can be helpful to anyone running Oracle on Windows.

Let's begin with a brief overview of the *net file* command.

The *net file* Command

This command is useful because it shows what remote users have files open on the server. While *tasklist /m* will show open .dll files, the *net file* command will show every file type. Again, this will only show files open by remote users, not local ones.

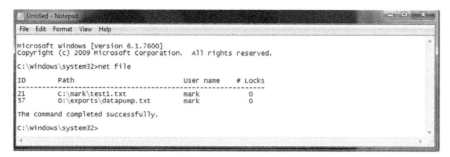

Figure 14.1: *Using the net file Command*

Windows 2008 UAC

Windows 2008 has a feature called User Account Control (UAC). In a nutshell, what it does is break the session token into a privileged and non-privileged token. By default, everything you do is done non-privileged unless you tell Windows differently.

This will require you to right click what you want to run and select *Run as administrator* for anything you wish to do that requires elevated access, even command prompt or explorer. You will need to check *Run with highest privileges* on batch jobs if they require privileges. UAC can be disabled if your IT Security allows it, but usually you need to live with it.

It is useful to run the command prompt as Administrator, which is done by right clicking the command prompt choice under Start/Programs/Accessories and choosing *Run as Administrator*. The top bar of the command prompt will tell you it is running as Administrator, as seen in Figure 14.2 below:

Figure 14.2: *Running the Command Prompt as Administrator*

Microsoft Technet has a good write-up on UAC here:

http://technet.microsoft.com/en-us/library/cc709691%28WS.10%29.aspx

ODBC on 64 Bit Machines

Sometimes you will need to run a 32bit application, such as Microsoft Access, on a 64bit server or client that requires an ODBC connection. If you simply run the Microsoft ODBC Administrator and add the datasource, your 32bit application will not see it.

To avoid this issue, you will need to run the 32bit Microsoft ODBC Administrator, which is located in the SYSWOW64 folder in your Windows software directory. For example:

```
C:\Windows\SYSWOW64\odbcad32.exe
```

It may also be necessary to use the 32bit Oracle Client ODBC software, which will work fine on a 64 bit machine.

Simple Table of UNIX to Windows Commands

UNIX	WINDOWS
cat	type, copy
cd	cd (plus if changing drives, type the drive letter first) e.g. C:>D: D:>cd D:\test
cp	copy, xcopy
cron	at, Task Scheduler
ftp	ftp
grep	find, findstr
ls	dir
man	help
mkdir	mkdir
more	more
mv	rename - to rename, move - actually move a file
netstat	netstat
nslookup	nslookup
ping	ping
ps	Task Manager, tasklist
pwd	cd
rm	del
rmdir	rmdir
telnet	telnet
traceroute	tracert
who	net session

What to do if an EXE Will Not Run

Sometimes you will have permissions to a shared folder and an executable, such as *setup.exe* in an Oracle Installation folder, but when you double click it, it will not run. This can be baffling, but there is a solution!

This can be done one of two ways:

1. You can remove Internet Explorer Enhanced Security from *Add and Remove Programs*. Internet Explorer Enhanced Security prevents exe files from running from a share, regardless of whether you are in the Admin Group or not.

2. From Internet Explorer, navigate to *Tools/Internet Options*, choose the *Security* tab, select *Internet*, and choose *Custom*. Then click the radio buttons for *Launching applications and unsafe files* to either *Enable* or *Prompt (recommended)*, as seen in Figure 14.3.

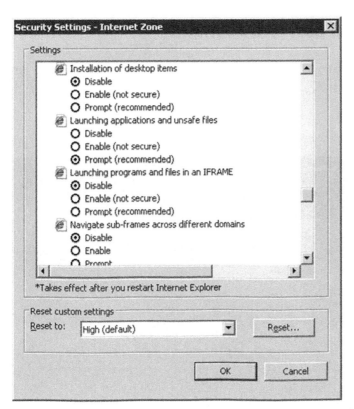

Figure 14.3: *Security Settings*

The *net statistics server* Command

The *net statistics server* command will return nodename, usage, error statistics, last start time, etc. for the machine, as seen in Figure 14.4 below.

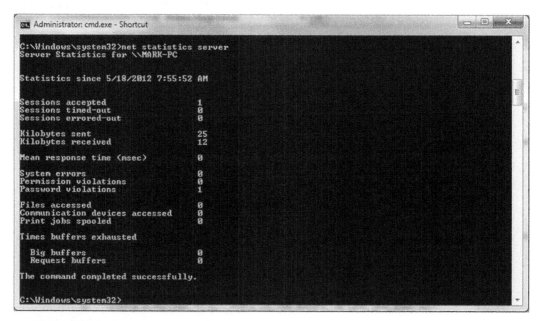

Figure 14.4: *The net statistics server Command*

The *systeminfo* Command

The *systeminfo* command will return basic hardware and operating system configuration information for the machine, as seen in Figure 14.5 below.

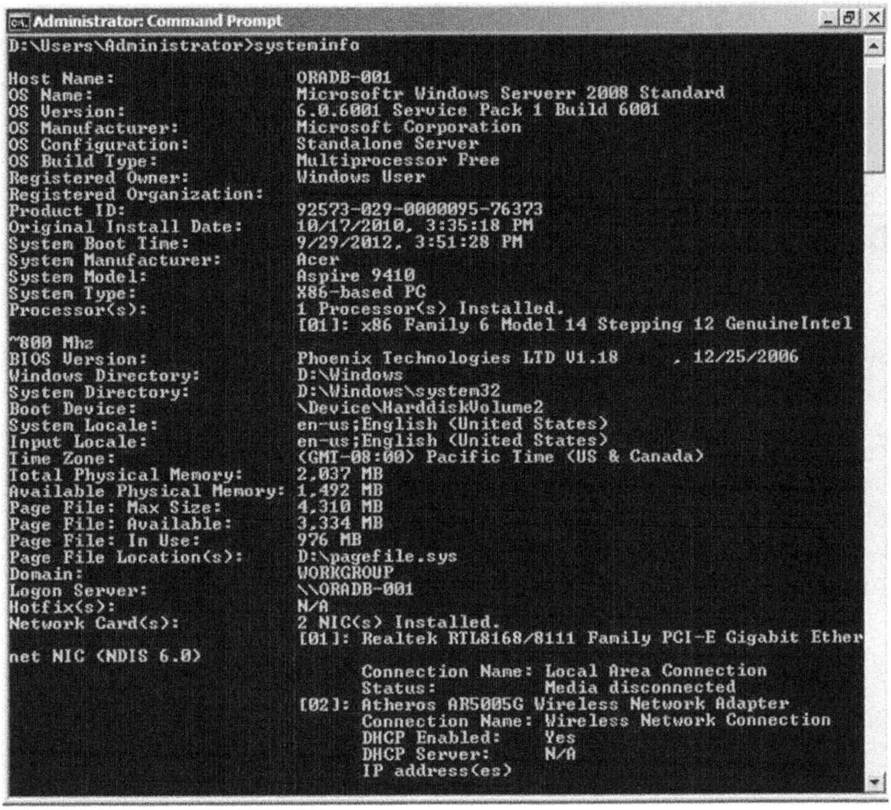

```
Administrator: Command Prompt                                         _ 8 X

D:\Users\Administrator>systeminfo

Host Name:                  ORADB-001
OS Name:                    Microsoftr Windows Serverr 2008 Standard
OS Version:                 6.0.6001 Service Pack 1 Build 6001
OS Manufacturer:            Microsoft Corporation
OS Configuration:           Standalone Server
OS Build Type:              Multiprocessor Free
Registered Owner:           Windows User
Registered Organization:
Product ID:                 92573-029-0000095-76373
Original Install Date:      10/17/2010, 3:35:18 PM
System Boot Time:           9/29/2012, 3:51:28 PM
System Manufacturer:        Acer
System Model:               Aspire 9410
System Type:                X86-based PC
Processor(s):               1 Processor(s) Installed.
                            [01]: x86 Family 6 Model 14 Stepping 12 GenuineIntel

~800 Mhz
BIOS Version:               Phoenix Technologies LTD V1.18     , 12/25/2006
Windows Directory:          D:\Windows
System Directory:           D:\Windows\system32
Boot Device:                \Device\HarddiskVolume2
System Locale:              en-us;English (United States)
Input Locale:               en-us;English (United States)
Time Zone:                  (GMT-08:00) Pacific Time (US & Canada)
Total Physical Memory:      2,037 MB
Available Physical Memory:  1,492 MB
Page File: Max Size:        4,310 MB
Page File: Available:       3,334 MB
Page File: In Use:          976 MB
Page File Location(s):      D:\pagefile.sys
Domain:                     WORKGROUP
Logon Server:               \\ORADB-001
Hotfix(s):                  N/A
Network Card(s):            2 NIC(s) Installed.
                            [01]: Realtek RTL8168/8111 Family PCI-E Gigabit Ether
net NIC (NDIS 6.0)
                                  Connection Name: Local Area Connection
                                  Status:          Media disconnected
                            [02]: Atheros AR5005G Wireless Network Adapter
                                  Connection Name: Wireless Network Connection
                                  DHCP Enabled:    Yes
                                  DHCP Server:     N/A
                                  IP address(es)
```

Figure 14.5: *Systeminfo Command Results*

Oracle Fail Safe

There is an option that comes with Oracle Enterprise Edition called Oracle Fail Safe. In brief, it allows Oracle to run on top of Microsoft Cluster software in an active/passive mode. If one server goes down, the other takes over. Both cluster members use the same disks, which are always connected to whichever cluster node is active. As this would take an entire book to explain how to install, configure, and run it, it is mentioned here for the sake of the reader's awareness!

Organizing Oracle Files – OFA on Windows

This assumes you are using the native Windows file system and not Oracle ASM. OFA stands for Optimal Flexible Architecture, and can be used on any Operating System, including Windows. The only thing to really consider is the resources available to you.

In general, one would want to place items that are written sequentially, such as Archivelogs (Flashback Recovery Area), Redo Logs, RMAN Backups, and Exports onto a RAID1 (Mirror Set) device.

For data files, ideally we would use RAID 10 (striped and mirrored).

However, many places do not wish to spend so much on spindles, so they use RAID5 or RAID6. There is a write penalty for using those, but it does protect the data.

The following is an example of OFA on Windows. Source: *Oracle Database Platform Guide 10g Release 1 for Windows*

```
C:\oracle\product    --First logical drive - Oracle Base
    \10.2.0              --Oracle home
      \bin                  --Subtree for Oracle binaries
      \network              --Subtree for Oracle Net
      \...
    \admin               --Subtree for database administration files
      \prod               --Subtree 'prod' database administration files
        \adhoc              --Ad hoc SQL scripts
```

```
        \adump              --Audit files
        \bdump              --Background process trace files
        \cdump              --Core dump files
        \create             --Database creation files
        \exp                --Database export files
        \pfile              --Initialization parameter file
        \udump              --User SQL trace files

F:\oracle                   --Second logical drive (RAID1)
    \oradata                --Subtree for Oracle Database files
      \prod                 --Subtree for 'prod' database files
        redo01.log          --Redo log file group one, member one
        redo02.log          --Redo log file group two, member one
        redo03.log          --Redo log file group three, member one

G:\oracle                   --Third logical drive (RAID 10,5, or 6)
    \oradata                --Subtree for Oracle Database files
      \prod                 --Subtree for 'prod' database files
        control01.ctl       --Control file 1
        indx01.dbf          --Index tablespace datafile
        rbs01.dbf           --Rollback tablespace datafile
        system01.dbf        --System tablespace datafile
        temp01.dbf          --Temporary tablespace datafile
        users01.dbf         --Users tablespace datafile

H:\oracle                   --Fourth logical drive
    \oradata                --Subtree for Oracle Database files
      \prod                 --Subtree for prod database files
        control02.ctl       --Control file 2
```

Comments on the Above

In the above example, *prod* is the SID of the database. Therefore, you can support multiple databases on the same devices. You could have *prod*, *prod1*, etc.

Please note the multiple Oracle Control Files. These can be very useful when one gets locked and/or corrupted.

Also please note the RAID level recommendations are just that – suggestions. Your mileage may vary depending on the hardware you have available and what you are using the database for.
Perhaps all the Server Admin will give you is one RAID5 drive for all of your Oracle Database files. Perhaps you want to mirror and stripe everything, or maybe the boss has sprung for a Solid State Disk Array.

The four drives in the example are just an example. If you have multiple terabytes and multiple devices, it would make sense to spread things out; heavily hit tablespace datafiles and indexes could be placed on separate devices. The idea is more keeping to the naming conventions than anything.

OFA is Oracle's way of standardizing directory structures so that you know where to find things in a consistent manner. In a multi-server environment, it is very beneficial to have all of the servers set up using the same directory structure. That way no matter which machine is being worked on, it is possible to go directly to whatever directories/folders needed without having to search. Consistency is a beautiful thing!

Summary

This chapter has covered several miscellaneous items, including the *net file* command, Windows 2008 UAC, ODBC, the *net statistics server* command, the *systeminfo* command, Oracle Fail Safe, and OFA on Windows. These commands and tips will hopefully prove useful to anyone using Oracle on the Windows platform.

Book Conclusion

And that, as they say, is that. If you got even one new helpful tip from reading this book, then it has been a success. Again, this was not intended to be a complete work on Windows Administration; that has been done many times before by individuals infinitely more qualified. Instead, this book has attempted to cover key portions of Windows that are of direct importance to an Oracle DBA. Through its pages, everything has been covered from a short history, to Oracle Installation tips, through scheduled tasks and shell scripting. These chapters are all meant to be springboards for further investigation and implementation; once you know something is possible and are pointed in the right direction, then truly the sky is the limit!!

Index

X

About the Author

Mark Sorger

Mark Sorger has 32 years of experience in IT. He began as an Application Programmer for Business Applications on RSTS/E and later VAX/VMS.

He moved on to VAX/VMS System Management, Windows Server administration, and Oracle Database Administration.

Mark has been an Oracle DBA for 17 years on VMS, Solaris, HP-UX, Windows, and Linux. He is currently the DBA Lead on a large Government Contract.

Lightning Source UK Ltd.
Milton Keynes UK
UKOW05f0626151115

262736UK00005B/39/P